KATHARINE HEPBURN

KATHARINE HEPBURN

A Pyramid Illustrated History of the Movies

by
ALVIN H. MARILL

General Editor: **TED SENNETT**

PYRAMID
PUBLICATIONS
NEW YORK

For patience—
above and
beyond the call.
To SANDY
and
JIM
and
STEVE

ISBN 0-515-02931-9

Library of Congress Catalog Card Number: 72-93665

Printed in the United States of America

Pyramid Illustrated History of the Movies

Published by Pyramid Publications, a division of Pyramid Communications, Inc. Its trademarks, consisting of the word "Pyramid" and the portrayal of a pyramid, are registered in the United States Patent Office.

PYRAMID COMMUNICATIONS, INC.
919 Third Avenue, New York, New York 10022

(graphic design by anthony basile)

PREFACE

By Ted Sennett

"The movies!" Flickering lights in the darkness that stirred our imaginations and haunted our dreams. All of us cherish memories of "going to the movies" to gasp at feats of derring-do, to roar with laughter at clownish antics, to weep at acts of noble sacrifice. For many filmgoers, the events on the screen were not only larger than life but also more mysterious, more fascinating, and—when times were bad—more rewarding. And if audiences could be blamed for preferring movies to life, they never seemed to notice, or care.

Of course the movies have always been more than a source of wish-fulfillment or a repository for nostalgic memories. From the first unsteady images to today's most experimental efforts, motion pictures have mirrored America's social history, and over the decades they have developed into an internationally esteemed art.

As social history, movies reflect our changing tastes, styles, and ideas. To our amusement, they show us how we looked and behaved: flappers with bobbed hair and bee-stung lips cavorting at "wild" parties; gangsters and G-men in striped suits and wide-brimmed hats exchanging gunfire in city streets; pompadoured "swing-shift" Susies and dashing servicemen, "working for Uncle Sam." To our chagrin, they show us the innocent (and sometimes not so innocent) lies we believed: that love triumphs over all adversity and even comes to broad-shouldered lady executives; that war is an heroic and virtually bloodless activity; that fame and success can be achieved indiscriminately by chorus girls, scientists, football players, and artists. To our edification, they show us how we felt about marriage in the twenties, crime in the thirties, war in the forties, big business in the fifties, and youth in the sixties. (Presumably future filmgoers will know how we felt about sex in the seventies.)

As an influential art, motion pictures are being studied and analyzed as never before by young filmgoers who are excited by the medium's past accomplishments and its even greater potential for the future. The rich body of films from *Intolerance* to *The Godfather;* the work of directors from Griffith to Kubrick; the uses of film for documenting events, ideas, and even emotions—these are the abundant materials from which film courses and film societies are being created across the country.

PYRAMID ILLUSTRATED HISTORY OF THE MOVIES also draws on these materials, encompassing in a series of publications all the people, the trends, and the concepts that have contributed to motion pictures as nostalgia, as social history, and as art. The books in the series range as widely as the camera-eye can take us, from the distant past when artists with a vision of film's possibilities shaped a new form of expression, to the immediate future, when the medium may well undergo changes as innovative as the first primitive movements.

PYRAMID ILLUSTRATED HISTORY OF THE MOVIES is a tribute to achievement: to the charismatic stars who linger in all our memories, and to the gifted people behind the cameras: the directors, the producers, the writers, the editors, the cameramen. It is also a salute to everyone who loves movies, forgives their failures, and acknowledges their shortcomings, who attends Bogart and Marx Brothers revivals and Ingmar Bergman retrospectives and festivals of forthcoming American and European films.

"The movies!" The cameras turn and the flickering images begin. And again we settle back to watch the screen, hoping to see a dream made real, an idea made palpable, or a promise fulfilled. On that unquenchable hope alone, the movies will endure.

CONTENTS

ACKNOWLEDGMENTS

Lewis Archibald, Alan Barbour, Mike Berman, John Cocchi, Guy Giampapa, Doug McClelland, Leo Pachter, Fred Romary, Bea Smith, Ted Sennett, Michael Schau, Chris Steinbrunner and
Apco-Apeda, Avco-Embassy, Cinerama Releasing, Columbia Pictures, Metro-Goldwyn-Mayer, Paramount Pictures, RKO Pictures, Twentieth Century-Fox, United Artists, Warner Brothers, and
Lincoln Center Library of the Performing Arts

KATHARINE HEPBURN once said: "What makes you a star is horsepower." The horsepower which has driven Hepburn for more than forty years in acting, for all of its open-throttle thrust and even its occasional sputtering and gear-shifting hesitation, has served well the self-lubricating, perpetual motion, uniquely-crafted, auburn-haired, and abundantly-freckled creation with the singleminded aim —to act. Hepburn today is one of the dwindling number among the great ladies of the Golden Days of the cinema still commanding star billing. And among the great ladies, she has been the most fiercely independent—and so were the ladies she portrayed on stage and on screen. They were the real feminists—the females of James M. Barrie and Philip Barry, the queens from Mary of Scotland to Eleanor of Aquitaine, the ambitious actresses of *Morning Glory* and *Stage Door,* the professional women and the spinsters, the dreamers and the realists. There were no women's libbers among them; her men were not male chauvinists. She never sought to prove she was better than any man—just his equal. She was a formidable rival as well as companion. Always, she remained a true individualist who could af-

INTRODUCTION

ford to go her own, self-chartered way.

"When I started out," she has admitted, "I didn't know I wanted to become an actress. I just wanted to be famous. And it wasn't until the movies that I knew what I really wanted—not to be just an actress, but a movie actress." In films—thirty-eight in four decades—she has been never less than the star, but, although she by-passed the normal starlet/B-picture/supporting role route, her career was a tooth-and-nail battle from the very beginning; among the combatants: virtually all of her directors (of whom only two or three survived the battle to work with and appreciate the lady's talents), each of the studios, most of her co-stars and some of her production crews. And as ambitiously as she has pursued her own ideas about acting, so has she stubbornly protected her privileges of privacy, her style of dress, her independent nature in general.

Her professional image has never been allowed to overshadow her individuality. Hepburn is never obscured by the role. Whether she is portraying a Jo March or a Clara Wieck Schumann or a Tracy Lord or a Mary Tyrone, there is always the special Hepburn quality that permeates the character and helps to mold a distinctive creation.

In his book, *Tracy and Hepburn*, Garson Kanin has written: "Katharine Hepburn has created, with diligence and intention, a world of her own, and she lives in it happily ever after. She is its Empress, its leading citizen, and the most common of its commoners. Her world has a Constitution (with the customary Amendments), laws, morals, and manners, sports, customs, two religions: Friendship and Behavior, tradition, policies, aims, and aspirations, a language, and—at the moment—even a population explosion."

Hepburn has permitted the world a look beyond the professional actress and at her private self at various times over the years. On one occasion, recalling her brief role as a wife, she admitted: "I was brought up surrounded by children. I am Aunt Kat—a lost generation. I never was a child and I never was a mother. I was Aunt Kat. I was my parents' friend, and I'm sure that's why I never really particularly wanted to get married."

And she has discussed her particular style of dress over the decades. "I found my cap in Germany between the wars, and I've had it copied over and over again. It's practical and chic and certainly comfortable. I wear a red sweater which I've had forever and is going to pieces on my back. I figure it will fall apart about the time I do. The fatigue jacket is something my brother once left behind. I wear slacks because I'm outdoors a lot. Besides, I don't give a damn how I dress. I never have."

Mostly, however, she limits her few comments to whatever interests her at the particular moment, and usually that is her most recent film. She sometimes expresses a fond remembrance of an earlier role; most often she prefers to let the roles she played stand on their own merit or live in the viewer's memory.

In this book, the stress will be on the Hepburn films and the actress' transformation on the screen from the aggressive, strong-willed young woman who is determined to remain independent in a man's world, to the lonely spinster in a wistful, even desperate, search for love.

In the final analysis, these films delineate the horsepower which has made Katharine Hepburn a star.

The basic biographical sketch of Katharine Hepburn reflects so typical a debutante that the facts well might have been simply excerpted from the society pages of the *Hartford Courant*. The lady's credentials are impeccable. There are intelligence, wealth, breeding. There is also a pair of remarkably distinctive traits—independence and rebelliousness. Since she decided to make acting her career, she has chosen to stress these traits, and it was her heavy reliance on them which became the catalyst for her rapid rise to stardom. Considering her track record of a frankly undistinguished parade of stage performances, capped by one middling success, her fantastic film career, spanning four decades, was lucky to have begun at all.

The head of the Hepburn family into which she was born on November 8, 1907, was Dr. Thomas Norval Hepburn, a transplanted Virginian who had been a Johns Hopkins graduate and was a prominent surgeon and chief urologist of the Hartford Hospital in Connecticut. His wife, Katharine, was a Boston Houghton, a graduate of both Bryn Mawr and Radcliffe, a suffragette and a crusader. "My mother," Katharine Hepburn (the younger) has declared,

THE STAGE YEARS

"was an emancipated woman; a fighter for her beliefs. I guess she'd be rated far left today, while my father was more conservative and would have been called a socialist. She was a pioneer in the birth control movement; she worked for it right alongside her friend, Margaret Sanger. In Hartford, that made her a dangerous and wicked woman." Mrs. Hepburn, one writer concluded, apparently believed in control of the children before birth and not afterwards. Her family name, Houghton, was proudly given as the middle name of each of her six children, of whom Katharine was the second.

The Hepburns are of Scottish descent, tracing the tree back at least to James Hepburn, the Earl of Bothwell, who was Mary Stuart's lover. In later years, when Katharine Hepburn played Mary Stuart in John Ford's *Mary of Scotland*, it is interesting that the name of James Hepburn was never mentioned. The role was enacted by Fredric March, referred to only as the Earl of Bothwell.

As a physical culturist, Dr. Hepburn instilled in his children a deep respect for good health, a competitive spirit and a love of sports. Katharine's tremendous physical drive in a wide variety of sports, ranging from wrestling to tennis, served her well in her acting career.

Like her brothers and sisters (Tom, who died in an accident at the age of twelve; Richard, now a playwright; Robert, a doctor; Marion, the mother of actress Katharine Houghton; and Peggy), Katharine was educated primarily at home by private tutors. Later, she attended Oxford School for Girls in Hartford, and, in 1924, entered Bryn Mawr, her mother's alma mater. As a child, Katharine took an interest in acting and, with a group of youngsters at the family's summer home at Fenwick on Long Island Sound, she formed a stock company, naming it the Hepburn Players. The fledgling actors staged various benefits and performed such heady works as *Bluebeard, Marley's Ghost,* and *Beauty and the Beast.*

Many years later, Hepburn wrote: "I had a remarkable upbringing and remarkable health. My parents were reformers and I was present and aware when they were doing things extremely advanced in such a conservative community. Not to be afraid to express your opinions, that's what they taught me. I was shunned at some parties, and it gave me a chip on the shoulder. But I always thought my parents were the greatest. I thought I was great, too. I didn't think I was pretty, though. I remember when I first went to Bryn Mawr. I walked into the dining room and somebody said, 'Self-conscious beauty.' I never went in there again."

At Bryn Mawr, Hepburn was not much of a student, but, thanks to Shakespearean scholar Horace Howard Furness, who chose her for the role of Pandora in an Elizabethan pageant entitled *The Woman in the Moone,* she became totally absorbed in acting—an ambition not wholeheartedly shared by the other Hepburns. Following graduation in 1928, she went to Baltimore with a letter of introduction to Edwin H. Knopf (later the noted MGM producer) whose stock company was home-based there. She hounded him until he finally took her on. The producer later said "I wanted no part of her, but it wasn't so easy to get rid of Hepburn." The tyro actress made her professional debut in Knopf's production of *The Czarina,* as a lady-in-waiting to its star, Mary Boland.

Then she appeared as a flapper in *The Cradle Snatchers,* in which Mary Boland again starred. Hepburn's independent approaches to these rather small roles began to run counter to the ideas of the plays' directors, and finally the company's stage manager, Kenneth MacKenna who later became head of the story department at MGM, advised her to obtain some professional training and to study voice under the noted coach, Frances Robinson-Duff. Hepburn did her detractors one better by also working on movement and dance with Michael Mordkin.

Miss Robinson-Duff has recalled her first sight of Hepburn: "It was raining. She had run up the stairs. She burst in the door, unannounced, and flung herself on the settee. Rain ran from her red hair and down her nose. She sat in a dripping huddle and stared. 'I want to be an actress,' she said. 'I want to learn everything.' The famed coach concluded that Hepburn did not know even the elements of acting and had only two gestures for her arms—held stiffly at attention like a soldier, or bent at the waist level with fists clenched. (Both are frequently demonstrated in many of her early films, most notably in *Morning Glory.*) One of Miss Robinson-Duff's prime concerns was controlling the Hepburn voice which was shrill when she was nervous, and she apparently was nervous all the time.

While in New York with Miss Robinson-Duff and with Mordkin, Hepburn learned that Edwin Knopf was coming to town to produce a play, *The Big Pond.* She went after a role in the play and was given the chance to understudy the leading lady. *The Big Pond* tried out in Great Neck, Long Island, where Hepburn suddenly found herself playing the female lead after the star was dismissed during rehearsals. Her opening night was a complete disaster as, through sheer nervousness, she accelerated her already rapid speech pattern (subsequently a distinctive Hepburn acting characteristic) to a point of utter unintelligibility and she began to flub her lines. She was fired shortly after the curtain descended.

Undeterred by her stage hysteria, she bounced back with characteristic resilience and finally opened on Broadway on November 12, 1928, following a series of tryouts, in *These Days.* (Although some sources list *Night Hostesses* as Hepburn's debut, there is no confirmation that she played a small part as one of the hostesses, under her own name.) *These Days* played only eight performances, but producer Arthur Hopkins then gave Hepburn the role of understudy to Hope Williams in Philip Barry's *Holiday,* which began its pre-Broadway tryout in New Haven.

Shortly after *Holiday* opened successfully on Broadway (November 26), Katharine Hepburn announced her intention to marry Ludlow Ogden Smith, a Philadelphia socialite and graduate of the University of Grenoble, who had been courting her while she was in college. Her grandfather, an Episcopal minister in Virginia, conducted the ceremony at the Hepburn home in West Hartford on December 12, 1928. She gave up her understudy role in *Holiday* and attempted to adjust to marital domesticity.

Since there already was one famous Kate Smith in show business, Hepburn rightly concluded that the world might not yet be prepared to accept a second. She convinced her husband to change *his* name by dropping the surname and reversing the other two. Yet even as Mrs. Ogden Ludlow, wife of a New York stockbroker, Hepburn found herself unwilling to accept her housewife role in a small East Side walk-up. Marriage, in fact, was interfering with her career. Luckily, the understudy role in *Holiday* was still open, and Arthur Hopkins took her back. Unluckily for Miss Hepburn however, Hope Williams never missed a performance.

The show closed the following June and the Ogden Ludlows went to Europe for a vacation. Hepburn was suddenly contacted to go on for Hope Williams, who had fallen ill during a road company tryout of *Holiday.* Hepburn went on—just once—as Linda Seton.

During her second season as an actress, Hepburn played three roles. They added up to exactly thirteen performances— and only five of these were on Broadway. She began by being fired during the Philadelphia tryout of Alberto Casella's *Death Takes a Holiday* in November, 1929. (Rose Hobart replaced her in the role of Grazia.) Hepburn had taken *Death Takes a Holiday* after previously accepting and then walking out on the ingenue role with the Lunts in S. N. Behrman's *Meteor* which the Theatre Guild was producing. It was only expediency years later, which forced the Guild to overlook this unpardonable action.

Hepburn then understudied

Eunice Stoddard and subsequently replaced Hortense Alden in the Guild's production of Ivan Turgenev's *A Month in the Country*. Frances Robinson-Duff next arranged for the young actress to get a summer of stock training with the Berkshire Players in Stockbridge, Massachusetts. Her spirit of renewed confidence apparently expanded into arrogance, and she reverted to form by squabbling with directors, authors, fellow performers, and whoever else was within range. In one of the plays, Hepburn was to step from the wings and call one of the characters. She insisted on calling the name of Laura Harding, her best friend in the company. The director protested, afraid that she might repeat on opening night what she insisted on doing in rehearsals: "Miss Hepburn, you just can't do that!" "Who's going to stop me?" Hepburn retorted. Otherwise, she kept insisting that she was the actress best suited for the lead in every production. She ultimately appeared in only two: G. Martinez Sierra's *A Romantic Young Lady* and Barrie's *The Admirable Crichton.*

As the new Broadway season was about to start, Hepburn was convinced that the New York stage was anxiously awaiting her return, and she obtained the role of Jane Cowl's daughter in Benn W. Levy's *Art and Mrs. Bottle.* The playwright immediately ran afoul of Hepburn's suggestions and soon had her fired. Unable to find a replacement as opening night approached, Levy was resigned to rehiring her at Miss Cowl's suggestion—and agreed to raise her salary. Hepburn received a number of good one-line notices from the New York press, and she made certain these did not go unread. She did one more season of summer stock, this time in Ivoryton, Connecticut.

In the fall of 1931, producer Gilbert Miller cast her as Daisy Sage opposite Leslie Howard in Philip Barry's *The Animal Kingdom.* Ilka Chase and William Gargan were also in the cast. Hepburn was dismissed from the production before the play reached Broadway. She has attributed her departure partly to her incompetence at the time and partly to the fact that she was taller than her leading man. This did not prevent her from venting her rage on author Philip Barry in a blistering telephone tirade.

The indomitable Miss Hepburn then indulged in her periodic renewal of strength in the bosom of her family. It has been

In ART AND MRS. BOTTLE (1930), with Jane Cowl

said that in her entire Broadway career, she never spent a Sunday in New York. Following the final Saturday night curtain, she always headed her car for Hartford.

Hepburn finally scored a Broadway success at the Morosco Theatre on March 11, 1932. As a prelude, the actress went through her customary routine of being fired and rehired, during rehearsals. The play, *The Warrior's Husband* by Julian Thompson, was a variation on the *Lysistrata* theme. She played Antiope, an Amazon queen who eventually succumbs to love, and made her entrance running down a thirty-foot stairway carrying a prop deer. Her costume, a bright tunic, showed off her slim figure and shapely legs, and later prompted her to say, with a slight touch of bitterness, "I never made a hit until I was in a leg show."

In *The Warrior's Husband*, Hepburn was called upon to toss her leading man, Colin Keith-Johnson, over her shoulder and, later, to wrestle him to the stage. The physical training her father had insisted upon years before,

16

As Antiope in THE WARRIOR'S HUSBAND (1932)

helped in her believable creation of the Amazon. The play itself will never be listed among legendary Broadway events, but Katharine Hepburn was able to assemble a portfolio of good notices, the most important of which was Brooks Atkinson's in the *New York Times:* "As Antiope, the Amazon who knows when she is beaten by love, Katharine Hepburn gives an excellent performance." She also got her first national notice when *Time* referred to her by name, identifying her as "a blonde, thin-cheeked girl."

Lillie Messenger, RKO Pictures' talent scout who worked out of New York, was one of those on whom Hepburn had made an impression in *The Warrior's Husband*. When word arrived at RKO's east coast office that David O. Selznick, head of production, was looking for somebody—preferably without screen experience—to star as Sydney Fairfield opposite John Barrymore in *A Bill of Divorcement*, a call was placed to Leland Hayward, Katharine Hepburn's manager.

Hepburn tested with a scene from *Holiday*, in which she naturally was letter perfect. It was filmed with Alan Campbell, who later married Dorothy Parker, as her foil—with his back to the camera. "I'd seen too many girls make screen tests with juveniles, only to have the juveniles hired," Hepburn later admitted. The test was shipped to the west coast and a wire was subsequently received by Leland Hayward with an offer from Selznick of five hundred dollars a week for his client's services.

Hepburn replied that she would prefer fifteen hundred dollars, which she was sure she would never get. In *The Warrior's Husband*, after all, she was making seventy-nine-fifty a week, and that had been cut from the hundred she earned when the show first opened.

Selznick wired a counter-offer: $1250 a week. Hepburn informed Hayward: "I said $1500 a week." Hayward finally suggested to Selznick, after deciding that his client would never give in, that the producer give her $1500 and she would give him a rehearsal week free. Thus Selznick would get his leading lady at a bargain rate ($6000 for the four weeks of production) and Hepburn would get a top per-week rate, and neither would have to compromise.

And that was how Katharine Hepburn became a movie star. Her contract guaranteed fifteen hundred a week for four weeks with options for five years encompassing five months a year; a promise that she would play the role of Sydney Fairfield; round-trip transportation; and a week off at the very beginning of the pact so that she could fulfill a previous engagement, performing in *The Bride the Sun Shines On* with a stock company in Ossining, New York.

Katharine Hepburn stepped off the train in Pasadena, California on Independence Day of 1932. A more apt date could not have been planned. The actress was prepared to challenge the film industry, but the industry may not have been ready for the actress. Both temperamentally and physically, she was hardly what the RKO brass thought they had hired. Producer Pandro Berman, who made many of her films both at RKO and at MGM, later described the Hepburn arrival. "She showed up at the RKO studio in a rented Hispano-Suiza that looked like a cross between a soda fountain and the Superchief. It was her idea of out-Hollywooding Hollywood. But the gag backfired. That particular car was known to every studio in town; we all had rented it for one picture or another. It had been Garbo's car in *Grand Hotel.*"

Out she sprinted, in her casual, mismatched, off-the-rack shirt-and-pants outfit—bizarre for the time, but subsequently traditional Hepburn. In over forty years in the public eye, the rule has been Hepburn in skirts only when called for in the script. A dress is professional wardrobe. ("I never could stand a dress," she has said. "I don't like stockings. I can't keep them

THE RKO YEARS

up. That's the first thing that started me wearing pants.") Next to her shrewd cash-register mind, her attire, soon to be part of the legend, was among the initial impressions the independent lady made on the film colony.

Although the front-office folk may have been dismayed by their newest acquisition ("My God," Myron Selznick was alleged to have said to his partner, Leland Hayward, on meeting Hepburn's train. "Did we stick David fifteen hundred for *that?*"), one person saw promise in the young actress. George Cukor, who had just directed his first film and had been assigned the screen version of *A Bill of Divorcement,* Clemence Dane's 1921 play, was astute enough to catch a special quality in her acting. Watching the *Holiday* test, Cukor was said to have been impressed by Hepburn's simple gesture of putting down a glass. Adela Rogers St. Johns wrote that he burst into her office: "I've just seen a test of the girl I want for *A Bill of Divorcement,*" he said. "She's too marvelous! She'll be greater

A BILL OF DIVORCEMENT (1932). With Billie Burke and John Barrymore

than Garbo! Nobody wants her but me, so come and help me fight for her. You don't need to see the test. It's a foul test anyhow. She looks like a boa constrictor on a fast. But she's great!" Cukor apparently was unaware at the time that Hepburn had been hired *specifically* to do *A Bill of Divorcement.*

Although she clashed with virtually everybody at the studio from her first day in Hollywood, Hepburn inexplicably warmed up to Cukor—after first berating him for her wardrobe—and they have remained fast friends

through the years, forming the only lasting actress/director association in her career.

A Bill of Divorcement (1932) remains a moving experience, both for the superb performance of John Barrymore and the outstanding debut of Katharine Hepburn. As a play, it elevated Katharine Cornell to stardom; as a film, it did the same for another Katharine. The critics were struck by Hepburn's angular face, her quicksilver personality, her distinctive voice. The *New York Times* critic, Mordaunt Hall, hailed her performance as "exceptionally fine . . . one of the finest characterizations seen on the screen."

In her role of Sydney Fairfield, Hepburn plays the daughter of a mentally tortured man, who forsakes her own happiness and gives up all thoughts of marriage to care for him. She fears that latent insanity runs in the family, after learning that her father (Barrymore) had escaped from the asylum to which he had been committed during the war. She had not known him until the day he returns home, as his wife (Billie Burke) is about to remarry. Barrymore's brilliant interpretation, which conveyed the desperate manner of an anguished man, was one of his best screen performances, but the film was dominated by the luminous if inexperienced Hepburn. The film's 1940 remake, with Maureen O'Hara, Adolphe Menjou and Fay Bainter, did nothing to obscure the brilliance of the original.

A Bill of Divorcement premiered in New York almost three months following Hepburn's arrival in Hollywood. RKO seemingly underestimated the actress' potential and the publicity department found itself totally unprepared for the film's success. It frantically attempted to conceal the fact that

A BILL OF DIVORCEMENT (1932). With Billie Burke

RKO knew as little about its new star as did the public. The futility of the department's press and public relations efforts rapidly became evident; the soon-to-be-legendary bouts Miss Hepburn had had with nearly every department on the lot were graphically duplicated. Her rudeness and insensitivity to others—from directors and fellow actors to lighting men and grips—were to characterize the first phase of her career in Hollywood. She immediately alienated the press by denying her marriage rather than simply refusing to discuss it; by playing games with interviewers,

A BILL OF DIVORCEMENT (1932). With David Manners

such as stating she had three children, only two of whom were white; by maintaining her outrageous attitude, even by the accepted Hollywood norm. But she was Katharine Hepburn. An independent.

Since it had a runaway hit on its hands, RKO was quite willing to overlook the Hepburn eccentricities. How to cash in on the commodity was the prime concern. A high-level suggestion was made to turn her into a Garbo.

And so, in her second film, Katharine Hepburn was painstakingly—and painfully—poured into a glamour girl mold with a silver-lame head-to-toe costume and a paint-crusted mouth. "The girl who set the world aflame in *A Bill of Divorcement*" was the line RKO placed below Hepburn's name in *Christopher Strong* (1933), the film which followed the actress' glorious debut. And the advertising department, forgetting when to quit, used this audience-grabbing catch phrase to promote the movie: "She tried to satisfy Desire (sic) with speed and thrills and danger!"

Christopher Strong, a vehicle originally intended for Ann Harding and Leslie Howard, is a dreary tale of illicit love among England's aristocracy. Dorothy Arzner, one of the few female directors in films, drew as good a performance from both Miss Hepburn and Colin Clive as possible, from Zöe Akins' adaptation of the Gilbert Frankau novel. When the film opened at New York's Radio City Music Hall, the first of seventeen *successive* Hepburn movies to play there, critic William Boehnel lamented in the *New York World-Telegram*: "She leaves some of us who cheered her along during her marvelous performance in *A*

CHRISTOPHER STRONG (1933). With Colin Clive

Bill of Divorcement aghast at the amateurish quality of her histrionics. For the first half of the film, she shrieks her lines in an unduly affected voice; for the rest of the time, her diction is so raspish, it jars the nerves."

Despite its inadequacy, Hepburn's performance as Lady Cynthia Darrington, the free-willed aviatrix, provided the first stage in her development of the screen's independent woman. Lady Cynthia first has an affair with Sir Christopher Strong (Clive), a married politician, causing no end of handwringing and consternation by his wife (Billie Burke) and his daughter (Helen Chandler). Then, while Sir Christopher tries to pick up the pieces of his disintegrating political career, Lady Cynthia flies off to the Riviera where she has a fling with an Italian romeo (Jack LaRue). Finally, seeing the error of her wicked ways, and finding herself pregnant, she decides to end it all by committing suicide at thirty thousand feet.

Critical opinion was mixed at best. Both the *New York Times* and the *Times* of London reviewed Hepburn's performance favorably, but public reception was disappointing. Her co-star Colin Clive had a few kind words: "She is not just a face,

MORNING GLORY (1933). With Adolphe Menjou

but a terrific personality. I said just now that she is not beautiful and that is true, though she understands the art of acting so amazingly that she can convey the illusion of beauty if the part demands it!"

While working on *Christopher Strong,* Hepburn received from Broadway producer Jed Harris the script to a British play he was preparing for the American stage. The play, called *The Lake,*

was a morbid psychological drama. She liked it, but RKO had a backlog of projects lined up for her. Jed Harris said that he would wait.

Zoë Akins' unproduced play *Morning Glory* became the source of the third Hepburn film. As aspiring young actress Eva Lovelace, she was playing a girl very much like herself, and Eva might well have been the Hepburn who had haunted

Edwin Knopf in his Baltimore office only a few years earlier. It might have been Hepburn herself in the film's opening sequence, as the star-struck girl walked slowly through the foyer of a theater gazing at the portrait gallery of theatrical luminaries—Ethel Barrymore, Maude Adams, John Drew, Sarah Bernhardt.

Hepburn's speeches in *Morning Glory* (1933), rattled off at breakneck speed (typifying much of her film work during this period), are perfect for the story, establishing her as a confident, brash young lady who fears that the professionals will cut her off should she ever stop talking. "My name's Eva Lovelace, that's my stage name, what's yours?" she asks the veteran actor, Robert Harley Hedges (C. Aubrey Smith), in the ante-room of noted producer Louis Easton (Adolphe Menjou). "You probably never heard of me. I'm just starting. I'm really Ada Love of Franklin, Vermont." And when she finally gets in to see Easton, with Hedges' help, and is asked her name, she breathlessly rattles

MORNING GLORY (1933). With Adolphe Menjou

off: "Eva Lovelace. Don't you like it? I can change it if you don't." Her progress is remarkably rapid in the theater, thanks in no small measure to an affair with Easton. Success, naturally, swells her head: "I'm gonna make you so proud of me—I'll be so wonderful!"

After creating a sensation by stepping in for the recalcitrant leading lady on opening night, she is fawned over by the stage crew, the producer, the director, and the playright (Douglas Fairbanks Jr.). Finally, it is Hedges who warns her not to succumb to her fame: "How many keep their heads? You've come to the fore. Now *you* have the chance to be a morning glory—a flower that fades before the sun is very high." And he turns his back on her, as does everybody else, as she vows: "I'm not afraid of being like a morning glory. I'm not afraid, I'm not afraid."

In the film, Hepburn gets the opportunity to do a soliloquy from *Hamlet* as well as the *Romeo and Juliet* balcony scene. And Menjou is asked to recite that immortal and often-repeated film line: "You don't belong to any man now—you belong to Broadway!" The critics were unanimous in their praise for the star; the film itself received lesser notices. It was de-scribed by one critic as *"Forty-Second Street* without music, dancing, or Ruby Keeler." Another thought there was "no purpose for the whole production except as a vehicle for the histrionics of Katharine Hepburn."

Her performance as Eva Lovelace—and many have maintained that her interpretation of Jo March in her following film weighed heavily in the decision —won Hepburn her first Academy Award. Thirty-four years would pass before she would win her second. *Morning Glory* was directed by Lowell Sherman, who doubtless came to battle well-armed, having previously worked with Mae West in *She Done Him Wrong.* In 1958, *Morning Glory* was again trotted out, under the title *Stage Struck,* as a vehicle to make a star of Susan Strasberg.

The fourth film for Hepburn, and her second directed by Cukor, was the screen classic, *Little Women* (1933). It was superbly adapted and lavishly mounted from the Louisa May Alcott story by Sarah Y. Mason and Victor Heerman, who won Academy Awards for their screenplay. The picture itself and director Cukor also received Oscar nominations. Hepburn was accorded sole above-the-title billing in this beautiful recrea-

LITTLE WOMEN (1933). With Frances Dee

tion of Civil War New England. In this sentimental tale of the March family, she played tomboyish Jo ("Look at me, world. I'm Jo March and I'm so happy!"), with Joan Bennett, Jean Parker, and Frances Dee as her sisters, and Spring Byington as her beloved Marmee. For her performance, which ranks among the highlights of her screen career, Hepburn was selected Best Actress at the 1934 Cannes Film Festival.

This version of the Louisa May Alcott novel was the second of three to be filmed. Dorothy Bernard was Jo in the silent version in 1919 and June Allyson attempted the part in MGM's Technicolor version in 1949. Selznick's own plans for a production with Jennifer Jones during the forties were abandoned.

Hepburn then expressed to the RKO brass her desire to return to Broadway in *The Lake* which Jed Harris was still holding for her. RKO agreed to let her go if she would first do one more film, *Spitfire,* for which they would pay her fifty thousand dollars.

The company required her services for only four weeks, and

LITTLE WOMEN (1933).
With Paul Lukas

LITTLE WOMEN (1933).
With Douglass Montgomery

the stop date was scheduled as November 15, 1933. Rehearsals for *The Lake* were to start on the sixteenth. At 6:15 on the afternoon of the fifteenth, when director John Cromwell called time, two scenes, including the ending, remained to be shot. Leland Hayward reminded the studio that his client's contract had expired, but the frontoffice shot back that the day was not over until midnight and that RKO was still entitled to five hours and forty-five minutes of the actress' time. On the sixteenth, then, Katharine Hepburn reported to the set of *Spitfire*. Shooting proceeded, but apparently nothing suited Crom-

well. At 3:45, in mid-scene, Hepburn stopped acting. The picture was still unfinished. A high-level conference was held in Pandro Berman's office. The actress had the studio over a barrel: since RKO had demanded and received its legal due, she simply was doing the same. She was asked her price for finishing the scene, which would be approximately one hour's worth of time. She demanded—and received—ten thousand dollars for her overtime.

From tomboy Jo March to tomboy Trigger Hicks is a long, long road. *Spitfire* (1934), following *Little Women*, provided Hepburn with the ill-advised role of a hellcat from the mountains of South Carolina, "a sad little thing," as the *New Yorker* put it, "given to prayer and savage rows with her neighbors." Headstrong and impulsive, Trigger is not above kidnaping a baby whose mother, she feels, is not fit to care for it. When the baby dies, the mountain folk try to stone Trigger to death, but she is rescued by a young engineer (Ralph Bellamy), who is taken with her for reasons difficult to fathom. Leaving on her enforced banishment from the community, she says to Bellamy: "Mr. Fleet, I reckon you can tell the folks I went a-prayin.' " Film critic Thornton Delehanty, writing in the *New York Post*, said: "Her Southern accent is pitched halfway between the Amos and the Andy of Amos 'n' Andy, and it is not more convincing than either."

Flying to New York, Hepburn then reported to Harris only twenty days before *The Lake* was scheduled to open. Harris himself was directing, having fired the man originally engaged. He, however, had been accustomed to working with experi-

SPITFIRE (1934). With Ralph Bellamy

SPITFIRE (1934). As Trigger Hicks

enced actors. The Hepburn technique of acting relied upon instinct. In little more than a week, director Harris nearly convinced Hepburn that she was not really an actress after all. The Dorothy Massingham-Murray MacDonald play opened for a single week in Washington, then on to New York. The star was well aware that her performance was still quite ragged. The critics had a similar opinion. One noted: "The second act's climax demanded high emotion from the leading woman. Miss Hepburn began the first act in full hysteria. By the time she reached her big moment, she could climb no higher. She was washed out." The famous Dorothy Parker barb, "She ran the gamut of emotion from A to B," remains the classic critical summation of Hepburn's performance in *The Lake*.

After fifty-five performances, the actress bought up her contract—it was the first time, but definitely not the last—for the $15,461.67 then posted in her checkbook. *The Lake* "dried up" on February 10, 1934. Before returning to Hollywood, Hepburn went to Europe to pick her Cannes Festival acting award, then on to Mexico to obtain a divorce from Ogden Ludlow, on May 9, 1934. With three disas-

ters out of the way—her film, her play, her marriage—Hepburn went back to RKO and signed for six more films during the next two years. She was paid $300,000.

Years later, speaking about her marriage, she said: "I behaved very badly. I was not fit to be married because I was fit to think only about myself. An actor, whose temperament as an actor tends this way, has to be very careful about getting married, because you're likely to make somebody else very unhappy." She concluded: "I don't particularly believe in marriage. It's an artificial relationship because you have to sign a contract. It's a guarantee that is made for the children, in hope that they will have a solid foundation."

Hepburn's first film in her new contract was *The Little Minister* (1934), James M. Barrie's wistful Scottish romance, which gave her the opportunity to mix her Bryn Mawr accent with a pronounced burr. In its ad campaign, RKO called the film its Christmas gift to the world, and billed its star simply as HEPBURN—in block letters twice the size of the title. Under her name: "More thrilling . . . More disturbing . . . More fascinating than ever!" And under

THE LITTLE MINISTER (1934). With John Beal

the title (and ahead of her co-stars), this legend was added: "Only the greatest actress of her time could have breathed life into the most magnetic heroine of all time!"

Katharine Hepburn plays Lady Babbie, the young and proper ward and prospective fiancée of Lord Rintoul (Frank Conroy), living in the town of Thrums in the Scotland of 1840. For her own amusement, she masquerades as a gypsy girl and involves herself with the labor turmoil of the town and with its humorless young cleric, Gavin Dishart (John Beal). Out of propriety

and shyness, he tries to fend off her flirtations, while she sees the opportunity for dominating him by playing on his emotions and finally extracing from him a proposal by putting words in his mouth. "Oh, if I were a man," she tells him, "I would wish to be everything that I am and nothing that I am. I would scorn to be a liar. I would choose to be open in all things. I would try to fight the world honestly. But I am only a woman, and so—well, that is the kind of man I would like to marry." Then she procedes to describe that man—brave, dominant, defiant, up-

32

THE LITTLE MINISTER (1934). With Beryl Mercer

holder of the weak, master of women. "He must rule me," says Babbie, "he must be my master." And Gavin says in subjugation, "Your Lord and Master . . . Babbie, I am that man!"

After getting "my little minister" to propose, she is obliged to have Lord Rintoul give up his prior claim on her. All is ultimately resolved when Gavin is seriously wounded during a weavers' strike in Thrums. The townsfolk, who had planned to ostracize their minister because of his assignations with the gypsy wench, forgive Gavin when they learn that the girl is Babbie. This heartfelt, Hepburn-style plea for the minister's life was typical of the dialogue which packed the romantics into New York's Radio City Music Hall where the film opened two days after Christmas of 1934: "Please, God, he is so good—he deserves your help—and they need him here in Thrums . . . and [with a breaking voice] dear God, I need him most of all."

Hepburn's Lady Babbie was compared rather favorably with the performance given by Maude Adams, the foremost Barrie interpreter, thirty-seven years earlier. André Sennwald, in the *New York Times*, wrote that she played the part "with likable sprightliness and charm." Richard Watts, Jr., critic for the *New York Herald-Tribune*, called Hepburn "one of the major wonder workers of Hollywood with an unconquerable gift for turning lavender and old lace into something possessing dramatic vitality and conviction."

The lovely adaptation of Barrie's story was by Sarah Y. Mason and Victor Heerman, who had won an Oscar for *Little Women*, and by Jane Murfin, who had worked on *Spitfire*. Previously, three silent film versions had been made of *The Little Minister*: in 1912 with Clara Kimball and two in 1921 with Betty Compson and Alice Calhoun.

The film that followed has always been considered the low point of Hepburn's RKO career. Teamed with Charles Boyer, the handsome Continental star whose American screen image was rapidly brightening, she starred in *Break of Hearts* (1935), one of the few original screenplays written for her. It was a banal tale of an eminent conductor who marries an aspiring young lady composer, a plot which has performed yeoman's service over the years. To promote the Hepburn-Boyer team, RKO's advertising department produced this catch phrase: "The star of a million moods *together* with the new idol of the screen."

The many Hepburn mannerisms were in abundance in *Break of Hearts*, especially the clenching and unclenching of her fists to denote shyness. And she made many references to her red hair and freckles. Finally, there were the now-customary trembling chin and brave smile preceding the flowing tears. Boyer tells her, in his smoothest manner: "Don't you know that you are a most exciting creature," to which Hepburn gushes: "I've loved you for such a long time. Since late this afternoon."

Shortly after their made-in-heaven marriage, she finds him having dinner with a former woman friend, while she herself is out with their own best friend (John Beal). Hepburn then walks out on Boyer, who proceeds to become a drunk with a ruined career. Beal tries to convince her to marry him, but she is unable to get her ex-husband out of her thoughts. When she at last locates him in a bar in an alcoholic stupor, she rushes to him and cries: "Oh my darling, it's not for what we were but for what we might have been," and

BREAK OF HEARTS (1935). With John Beal and Charles Boyer

then goes to the piano to play her concerto for him. He emerges briefly from his stupor, then collapses. At the fade out, he is once again a respected conductor, having been nursed back to health by a forgiving wife. The soap-opera style screenplay for *Break of Hearts* was by Sarah Y. Mason and Victor Heerman, working on their third successive Hepburn movie, this time with Anthony Veiller. Stage director Philip Moeller, who had come to Hollywood the previous year to work with Irene Dunne in *The Age of Innocence*, returned to Broadway after directing Hepburn in *Break of Hearts.*

After *Break of Hearts*, the actress' career could only improve. Happily, her next film was an exhilarating success and one of the best films she made at RKO. Hepburn had suggested to the studio that she do Booth Tarkington's *Seventeen.* RKO countered with the author's 1921 Pulitzer Prize-winning *Alice Adams,* giving her a minor director named George Stevens, whose previous experience had been on Wheeler and Woolsey slapstick comedies. From Hep-

BREAK OF HEARTS (1935). With Charles Boyer

burn, he extracted a touching performance equal to her Jo March, and winning her a second Oscar nomination. The film itself was also nominated.

In the title role, Hepburn plays a lovesick young girl attempting to compete on an equal level with socially superior acquaintances and to impress the handsome young man (Fred MacMurray) she had met at the dance. Her own meager circumstances are beautifully established in the film's opening scenes. Hepburn stops at the local florist to buy herself a cor-

sage for the dance, but finding the cost prohibitive, she picks a bunch of violets in the public park. Then she must weather the social embarrassment of being escorted to the party by her reluctant brother (Frank Albertson).

Sometime later, meeting Mac-Murray on the street, Hepburn rattles on about the family's nonexistent wealth, about the problems of hiring secretaries for her father (who is out of work), about her dancing and acting talents. As they walk, she begins to recite Shakespeare and delib-

BREAK OF HEARTS (1935). With Charles Boyer

erately passes her house, too ashamed to invite MacMurray in to meet her parents.

Following a number of dates—always *outside* the house—she is finally obliged to invite him to dinner, and she convinces her parents to hire a maid for the occasion. The highlight of the film —indeed one of the best-remembered moments in films of that era—is the dinner party, "stolen" by Hattie McDaniel as the slatternly maid, Malena. She grumbles over the menu, battles balky dining room doors, fights a flopping maid's cap, chews gum,

and shuffles her way through a series of unappetizing courses. Hepburn soon realizes that the dinner is a disaster and that MacMurray is quite ill-at-ease. When her brother interrupts the meal for an urgent talk with their father (Fred Stone), Hepburn maneuvers MacMurray out of the house, where they both sheepishly search for words. She finally tells him: "You know, I have a strange feeling. I feel as though I'm only going to see you for five minutes more in my whole life." Then, she runs back into the house to help settle fam-

ALICE ADAMS (1935). With Ann Shoemaker, Fred MacMurray, Hattie McDaniel and Fred Stone

ily money problems. MacMurray is waiting for her, much to her surprise, when she again walks outside.

Production on *Alice Adams* was far from easy. The star and the director maintained a "Miss Hepburn" and "Mr. Stevens" relationship for weeks. In attempting to shoot the scene where Alice's boyfriend leaves after the family dinner, director Stevens insisted that she turn on the tears at the window rather than on the bed as the script called for. "I'll cry on the bed," the star is said to have insisted. It soon became a standoff. Finally Stevens shouted: "Either

you'll cry at the window or I'll return to my custard pies!" To which Hepburn retorted: "A quitter! If I ever had any respect for you, it's now gone! You don't get your way, so you quit! You're yellow!"

Stevens then suggested this compromise: "Miss Hepburn, just walk to the window, please, and stand there awhile. You needn't weep. I'll dub someone in, in a long shot, and we can fake the sound track." She walked to the window—and wept.

Another crying incident in the same film involving the screen's greatest "on cue" weeper oc-

ALICE ADAMS (1935). With Fred MacMurray

ALICE ADAMS (1935). With Fred MacMurray

curred in the scene where Alice's father, unaware that his daughter's date had been less than successful, comes into her room and says: "That young man tonight was the nicest you've ever brought home!" The script calls for Hepburn to begin crying on her father's last word. George Stevens mentioned: "It would be a blessing if you could manage a tear on cue. Try it once, will you? If you can't bring it off, we'll use glycerin." The cameras rolled, and exactly on the word "home," a tear fell. The cameraman then told Stevens that the lighting was wrong, and Hepburn insisted on shooting it once again. Again her tears fell exactly on cue. Stevens decided to press his luck with yet another take, and once more the Hepburn tears began to roll. The director, long since a good friend of his leading lady, some time later admitted never having seen anything like that "on demand" performance, before or since.

To Hepburn, the scene was nothing out of the ordinary. She confided: "Pop was played by Fred Stone, who was so sweet— he looked like a helpless baby lion, you know— I could have cried fifty times."

Although *Alice Adams* is rather hackneyed by today's

SYLVIA SCARLETT (1936). With Edmund Gwenn

SYLVIA SCARLETT (1936). With Cary Grant and Edmund Gwenn

SYLVIA SCARLETT (1936). With Brian Aherne

story standards, the film was a great success, primarily because of the exceptional performances of Hepburn and Fred Stone (in his first sound movie) and of the brilliant bit by Hattie McDaniel. *Alice Adams* had been filmed once before—as a 1923 silent movie with Florence Vidor.

The Hepburn-Cukor combination next worked on *Sylvia Scarlett* (1936), a film version of the 1918 Compton MacKenzie novel, *The Early Life and Adventures of Sylvia Scarlett*. Its offbeat story of a young girl who masquerades as a boy and becomes involved with a gang of vaga-

bond thieves in London was dull and foolish, and the film was liked by neither critics nor public. Following one disastrous sneak preview of the movie, Hepburn and Cukor allegedly each offered to do a picture without pay if RKO would scrap this one. The studio, however, refused, claiming that it could not afford the loss of production costs.

Time magazine noted in its review: "*Sylvia Scarlett* reveals the interesting fact that Katharine Hepburn is better looking as a boy than as a woman." André Sennwald summed up his impressions of the film in the *New York Times:* "Probably it is unkind to say of *Sylvia Scarlett* that it begins at 12:00 sharp and ends at 1:40. And yet that is precisely its total effect."

Among the few positive results of *Sylvia Scarlett* was the impetus it gave to the career of Cary Grant, particularly in light comedy. On loan from Paramount, Grant drew the film's best notices for his portrayal of the cockney crook, Jimmy Monkley. It marked the first of four Hepburn-Grant screen teamings.

The ultimate failure of Katharine Hepburn to capture the public's fancy (and to replenish the RKO coffers) during the thirties was laid on the studio's doorstep by producer Pandro Berman himself. Writing about Hepburn in June, 1947, Berman stated: "Kate's career was having its ups and downs. Who was to blame? Well, we were, primarily. Kate was RKO's biggest individual star. She and the team of Astaire and Rogers were the backbone of the studio. We turned out so many Hepburn pictures every season—right or wrong, ready or not ready. But there was another factor. We hadn't found Kate's right formula. I don't mean that she is limited or has to be typed. But that a certain character line

suits her best. And that line happened to correspond to Kate's own character. She can't be namby-pamby or stickily sentimental. She has to have a certain arrogance which audiences like to see humbled, but without breaking her spirit."

Hepburn was obliged to turn down an offer from Max Reinhardt to play Viola in *Twelfth Night* at the Hollywood Bowl because RKO had scheduled her to play the lead in *Mary of Scotland* (1936), the first of three successive costume dramas. Appearing opposite Fredric March as James Hepburn, the Earl of Bothwell, and Florence Eldridge as Queen Elizabeth, Katharine Hepburn made her only film with director John Ford, for whom this was rather an off-beat assignment, and gave an elegant interpretation of Mary Stuart. Ford had put Dudley Nichols to the task of adapting Maxwell Anderson's 1933 play to the screen, and Nichols created a colorful and stirring— although, as most critics agreed, static—scenario.

The actress worked hard at the role, but the Mary Stuart both of legend and of playwright Anderson was at definite odds with her own personality. She seemed ill at ease delivering such speeches as: "I too have a

MARY OF SCOTLAND (1936). With Fredric March

43

MARY OF SCOTLAND (1936).
With John Carradine

will, a will as strong as your own, and enemies of my own and my long revenges to carry through. I will have my way in my time though it burn my heart out and yours. The gods set us tasks, my lord, what we must do!"

Although *Time's* reviewer wrote: "Katharine Hepburn acts like a Bryn Mawr senior in a May Day pageant," the *New York Times* film critic, Frank Nugent, was somewhat kinder, saying: "Although (her) Mary Stuart shines brilliantly through most of the film's two-hour course, we were conscious of definite defects in her characterization. She may be a coura-geous Mary, perhaps a valiant one, but scarcely a fighter who gives no quarter and asks none."

Much was made of the historically inaccurate meeting of the two queens, devised by Maxwell Anderson claiming poetic license, but it was an effective scene, with Hepburn and Eldridge striking sparks as formidable adversaries facing harsh realities.

The role which followed Hepburn's Mary Stuart undoubtedly must have been close to the heart of the actress' mother; it dealt with a woman's struggle for emancipation during the Victorian period. Hepburn played the defiant Pamela Thistlewaite in *A Woman Rebels* (1936), the film version of Netta Syrett's *Portrait of a Rebel*. Pamela's rebellion against the social mores of late nineteenth-century England includes defiance of her autocratic father (Donald Crisp), pregnancy out of wedlock with her lover Gerald Waring (Van Heflin, in his screen debut), and independence by raising her illegitimate daughter as her niece. Ultimately she achieves strength through self-support as a crusading journalist and marries gallant young diplomat Thomas Lane (Herbert Marshall), after protecting him from the stigma of her youthful indiscretion with

A WOMAN REBELS (1936). With Van Heflin

Gerald. *A Woman Rebels* was pure soap opera, albeit sumptuously mounted, and Hepburn's performance as the defiant young woman remains the epitome of her feminist characterizations of the 1930s.

Hepburn is credited with bringing to films both Van Heflin and Doris Dudley (as Pamela's grown daughter in *A Woman Rebels*). It was at the star's insistence that both were given roles in this movie. It was also through Hepburn's persistence that Van Heflin continued his career, obtaining for him the role of Macaulay Connor, the reporter in the stage version of *The Philadelphia Story,* after he became discouraged in Hollywood following a series of minor films at RKO.

Quality Street (1937), another costume piece of Victorian England, came next in Hepburn's career. Working again with director George Stevens and again in a James M. Barrie story, she played Phoebe Throssel in another stylish soap opera about a young romantic who, when her doctor boyfriend (Franchot Tone) sails off to the Napoleonic

QUALITY STREET (1937). With Franchot Tone

Wars, turns into a faded, spinsterish schoolmarm like her older sister (Fay Bainter). When the doctor returns ten years later, Phoebe resorts to trickery —masquerading as her own imaginary coquettish niece—to lure him back when she thinks his affection has cooled over the decade. Her performance was not well received by the *New York Times.* Frank Nugent wrote in his review: "Her Phoebe Throssel needs a neurologist far more than a husband. Such flutterings and jitterings and twitchings, such hand-wringings and mouth quaverings, such runnings about and eyebrow-rais-

ings have not been seen on the screen in many a moon." Most critics, however, found this Barrie heroine more to Hepburn's style than her Babbie of *The Little Minister,* and her portrayal of Phoebe provided glimpses of many of the spinsterish roles she was to undertake later in her career. (The screen's previous Phoebe Throssel was Marion Davies in 1928.)

On completing *Quality Street,* Hepburn was released from RKO, and decided to return to the stage. She accepted an offer from the Theatre Guild to star in a new adaptation of Charlotte Bronte's *Jane Eyre.* First, of course, there was a monetary hassle to be ironed out. The Guild offered a thousand dollars a week. Hepburn countered with a figure half again as much. Her contention was that the overage was sort of blood money for humiliations she considered she had suffered as an ingenue at the hands of the Guild. A settlement was reached—in Hepburn's favor, naturally.

Jane Eyre opened in New Haven on Christmas Day, 1936. Mixed reviews caused the producers to alter their plans for bringing the show to Broadway. Instead, they scheduled an extensive tour which skirted New York and ended in Bal-

QUALITY STREET (1937). With Roland Varno and Joan Fontaine

QUALITY STREET (1937). With Franchot Tone and Fay Bainter

STAGE DOOR (1937). With Ginger Rogers

Morrie Ryskind and Anthony Veiller, the focus and characters were altered (in some cases, drastically), and, sin of all sins, one of the other female roles was built up at the expense of Hepburn's. Playwright Kaufman was said to have scoffed, "Why didn't they call it *Screen Door?*"

In Hepburn's mind, the battle lines had been drawn, the challenges clear. Playing Terry Randall, a smug young debutante and actress who lands an important Broadway role because her father has secretly backed the play, she gave a far better performance than RKO and even the Hollywood community had expected. *Stage Door* (1937) deals with a group of would-be actresses, living in The Footlights Club, a theatrical rooming house, while awaiting that big break. Hepburn, as the dilettante, moves in "for the atmosphere," after leaving home to make her own mark. "If I can act, I want the world to know it," she says. "If I can't act, *I* want to know it." Neither hiding nor flaunting her wealth or her superiority, she makes a resolute effort to fit in as one of the girls, such as rooming with a flippant, cynical dancer (Ginger Rogers) with "an inferior upbringing" (Terry's observation).

Terry gradually endears her-

timore early the following April —five days before Hepburn's most recent film, *Quality Street* went into release. On the actress' return to Hollywood, RKO negotiated a new four-picture contract with her. Only two were ever made. When she received the script to *Stage Door,* she was expecting to do the screen version of the Edna Ferber-George S. Kaufman Broadway comedy. But after having paid $125,000 for the screen rights, RKO promptly dropped the Ferber/Kaufman material, retaining only the title and the skeletal framework. In the screenplay, fashioned by self to the girls in the house—her roommate, of course, is the last to come around—and proceeds to become a confidante of each. An aging actress (Constance Collier) offers to coach Terry who, like the others, makes the rounds of producers' offices and tries to bluff them with nonexistent experience. When one producer, Anthony Powell (Adolphe Menjou), makes a play for Terry's roommate, after arranging a dancing job in a posh club he owns, Terry breaks up the relationship by going to his apartment and making certain she is found there in a compromising position by Jean. Powell, realizing he has met his match in Terry, gives her the lead in his new play, for which her father is the secret angel. It is the role Kaye Hamilton (Andrea Leeds), a dedicated young ingenue who also lives at the club, had hoped to land.

The totally inexperienced Terry immediately begins making staging suggestions during rehearsals (shades of an earlier Katharine Hepburn!), imposing herself on everyone associated with the play. On her opening night, before leaving for the theater, she is visited by Kaye, who gives her a few constructive comments on how the role might best be interpreted and how

STAGE DOOR (1937). With Adolphe Menjou and Ginger Rogers

Terry should carry the flowers on her entrance speech. Then, when the other girls have left for the opening of the play, Kaye jumps out of a window. Learning of the suicide as she is about to make her entrance, Terry is shattered, but nevertheless proceeds to give a moving performance with new meaning to her lines (which were to become identified with Hepburn for many years): "The calla lilies are in bloom again. Such a strange flower—suitable to any occasion. I carried them on my wedding day; now I place them here in memory of something that has died."

Naturally, Terry is a sensation

—and a new star. Following the play, which was modeled closely on a scene from Hepburn's 1933 play, *The Lake,* Terry gives a dramatic curtain speech, reducing her actress friends in the audience to tears: "The person you should be applauding died a few hours ago . . . I hope that wherever she is she knows and understands and forgives." She and Jean then race off to the morgue to view Kaye's body, but only after Terry receives those now-familiar words from her dramatic coach: "You're an actress now—you belong to these people." Note the similarity to the lines spoken by Menjou to Hepburn in *Morning Glory.*

Hepburn's emotional curtain speech at the climax ran four pages in the original script. Director Gregory La Cava, for whom, it has been said, a script exists only to be ignored, cut the speech to a mere ten lines. From then on, Hepburn was on her own. La Cava closed the set to all—including the rest of the cast. His plan was to show the effect of the speech on the theater audience. Then he brought in the extras and played it back. "Many of them wept," he said later, "and their faces were sufficiently moved to give me what I wanted." And then Ginger Rogers came in—and wept.

"The only way I'd ever been able to get her to cry before was to tell her her house was burning down." La Cava won the New York Film Critics' Award as Best Director for *Stage Door.* He had this appraisal of Hepburn: "She is completely the intellectual actress. She has to understand the why of everything before she can feel; then, when the meaning has soaked in, emotion comes—and superb work."

Not only was Hepburn superb in *Stage Door* but Ginger Rogers proved herself a first-rate comedienne. However, despite competition from a strong cast which included such talented players as Gail Patrick, Lucille Ball, Eve Arden, Ann Miller, Jack Carson, and Franklin Pangborn (in another of his marvelous bits as Menjou's effete butler), *Stage Door* was stolen by Andrea Leeds as Kaye. She had been borrowed by RKO from Samuel Goldwyn for the role, and received an Academy Award nomination as Best Supporting Actress for her performance. Her brief screen career ended not long afterwards, with her retirement from films in 1940 at the age of twenty-six. In addition to her Oscar nomination, *Stage Door* also was nominated for Best Picture, Best Director, and Best Screenplay.

Because of the enthusiastic response to *Stage Door,* RKO began to consider that perhaps Katharine Hepburn had a flair for comedy they had not yet tapped. She was then cast opposite Cary Grant in Howard Hawks' *Bringing Up Baby* (1938), a frantic romp which was among the last of the decade's fondly remembered screwball comedies. The film provided Hepburn with her first attempt at this highly specialized art, and *Time* acknowledged: "She can be as amusingly skittery a comedienne as the best of them."

As Susan Vance, she is a scatterbrained heiress (with a mind like a trap, as it turns out) who gets what she wants—and what she wants is stodgy, bespectacled David Huxley (Grant), a paleontologist who is preoccupied with locating the remaining bones of the Brontosaurian skeleton he has been recreating. The dizzy debutante keeps insisting that everything in sight belongs to her: David's golf ball, David's car, David. She embarrasses him publicly in her own flighty way, causes pandemonium in a restaurant—first through a mixup of purses and then by ripping the back of her gown, forcing David to "walk" her out of the room "in tandem" —and blackmails him into car-

ing for her pet leopard (the "Baby" of the title), which enjoys being serenaded to the strains of "I Can't Give You Anything But Love." Hepburn prattles her zany way through 102 frenetic minutes—bent on jamming in what seems to be 120 minutes worth of dialogue. Grant, however, gets most of the good lines. There is, for example, the episode in which Grant is wearing one of Hepburn's negligees after she has sent his clothes to the cleaners. Suddenly confronted by her formidable aunt (May Robson), he responds to her queries about his attire: "Because I just went gay all of a sudden."

Throughout the film, it is Hepburn who is the dominant figure, leading Grant around, accepting no responsibility for any embarrassment she causes him, humiliating him constantly. Only at the end of *Bringing Up Baby,* after Grant returns to his own milieu and the companionship of his jigsaw of a skeleton, does he exert his male authority. Hepburn, if she wants him, must come up to him—on his scaffold.

With *Bringing Up Baby,* Katharine Hepburn ended her days as RKO's top star. Considered "box office poison" by the Theater Owners of America (al-

BRINGING UP BABY (1938). With Cary Grant

BRINGING UP BABY (1938). With Cary Grant and Billy Bevan

164

though most of her films were first-rate and well-received), the actress bought out her contract with the studio rather than subject herself to professional humiliation in a minor film which RKO offered her (*Mother Carey's Chickens*, made subsequently with Anne Shirley and Ruby Keeler). It cost her two-hundred thousand dollars to leave, and she even forgot about collecting the twenty thousand due her in overtime.

Before closing this first phase of her film career, the actress drew upon her innate business acumen to negotiate a one-picture deal with Columbia after learning that they had obtained the rights from RKO to the Philip Barry play, *Holiday*. She convinced Harry Cohn that she *had* to play Linda Seton in this version, that only George Cukor could direct her, and that Cary Grant would be perfect as Johnny Case. Cohn signed her and gave her $175,000, which was $25,000 more than RKO had been paying her per picture. In *Holiday*, she gave one of her best screen performances, making the role her own and creating this version as a first-rate comedy of manners.

Author Philip Barry's longtime friend, Donald Ogden Stewart, who, as an actor, had played Nick Potter in the stage version of *Holiday*, collaborated with Sidney Buchman on the screenplay. (George Cukor recently divulged that credit should go to Stewart alone and that Buchman's name was there because of studio politics.) Polishing and updating (from the twenties to the thirties) the sophisticated comedy, Stewart (and Buchman) turned Linda Seton into the very epitome of Hepburn: rich, literate, rebellious. Linda is the unconventional older sister who is completely out of sympathy with the values of her conservative banker father (Henry Kolker). She also disrupts the marriage plans of her snobbish sister (Doris Nolan) to non-conformist Johnny Case—or Chase, as the girls' father calls him because, Linda says, "Chase has such a sweet banking sound." Linda encourages Johnny's off-beat plan to retire young, live his life as an extended holiday, and *then* go to work.

Linda and Johnny meet for the first time, shortly after he discovers that the Setons are fabulously wealthy, and she assures him that the house is actually haunted—by ghosts wearing "stuffed shirts and mink-lined ties." They are immediately drawn to one another by their

HOLIDAY (1938). With Doris Nolan, Cary Grant and Lew Ayres

complete candor, and from then to the end it's girl meets boy, girl loses boy, girl gets boy—and, in this case, society and the entire social register be damned. As Linda, who is in total agreement with Johnny's holiday concept, finally admits: "Oh, I've got all the faith in the world in Johnny. Whatever he does is all right with me. If he wants to sit on his tail, he can sit on his tail. If he wants to come back and sell peanuts, Lord, how I'll believe in those peanuts!"

Deftly amusing and gracefully played, *Holiday* succinctly captured the thirties' cinema concepts of society and life among the idle rich. On the stage, where it had first played just before the Wall Street crash, *Holiday* had been viewed rather differently—as a satire of the rich and a criticism of the mindless accumulation of wealth. This was the second film version of the Barry play. Pathé, the predecessor of RKO, had made a version in 1930 with Ann Harding in the Linda Seton role receiving an Academy Award nomination for her performance.

Like every actress in Hollywood, Katharine Hepburn had been angling for the Scarlett O'Hara role in *Gone with the Wind* and had a strong ally in George Cukor, the original director of the Selznick epic. The actress first became aware of the Margaret Mitchell book while in the east touring in *Jane Eyre*. Lillie Messenger, the RKO talent scout who had made Hepburn's screen test in 1932, had read the galleys of the unpublished novel, thought Hep-

HOLIDAY (1938). With Cary Grant

burn would be ideal for Scarlett, and took a short option on the property on behalf of RKO. She sent copies to Hepburn, to Pandro Berman, and to RKO president Leo Spitz. Berman allegedly was less than enthusiastic, believing that costume dramas were going out of style. Although Hepburn argued valiantly with Spitz for the project, it was Berman who convinced him that the price—fifty-two thousand dollars —was too high! RKO withdrew its bid. Hepburn then went directly to David O. Selznick, now an independent producer, who had bought the rights to the book. There are various stories about their meeting. Supposedly, Selznick would not commit himself after hearing her plea for the role, but he offered to test her. She refused, arguing: "You know what I look like on the screen. You know I can act. And you know that this role was practically written for me. I *am* Scarlett O'Hara!" Selznick was said to have shot back: "I just can't imagine Clark Gable chasing you for ten years." To which a furious Hepburn retorted: "I may not appeal to you, David, but there *are* men with different tastes!"

So after finishing *Holiday*, and considering and then rejecting other offers because she could not have script approval, the actress packed up and went East to Fenwick. She had made fifteen movies in Hollywood, and her hard-edged New England determination gave hope to the film colony that she would be heard from soon again.

A long-distance phone call to Fenwick from playwright and friend Philip Barry marked the turning point in Katharine Hepburn's career. She had appeared in two of his plays: as Linda Seton in *Holiday* and as Daisy Sage in *The Animal Kingdom*. Barry himself had not had a successful play since *The Animal Kingdom* in 1931. He suggested that perhaps another association between them might prove beneficial. He had an idea for a play which he would like to discuss with her and could he come up to Connecticut?

Hepburn and Barry picnicked while the playwright read her part of his new comedy. It was to deal with a spoiled rich girl on the eve of her second marriage. The leading lady was named Tracy Lord; the play was called *The Philadelphia Story*.

Nearly twenty years later, Hepburn discussed the problems of getting the play produced. "When I was very young," she recounted, "I used to be arrogant and—well, quite arrogant, rather like the girl I played in *The Philadelphia Story*. Phil Barry wrote that for me. I had been a movie star up to then, but my career was already over. I was labeled box-office poison. So I got Phil to say he would let the Theatre Guild produce the

play, and I got them to let me be the only one in contact with Phil, who was still writing it. I didn't know the Guild was in money trouble. *They* didn't know I was finished in Hollywood. *Phil* didn't know about anything, and *I* didn't know Phil had no idea for a third act. It just all worked, and it made me a star again."

The actress and the author each put up one-fourth of the cost of production and the Theatre Guild managed to find enough funds in its nearly depleted coffers to buy another fourth of the play—which, ultimately, helped bail out the Guild. Word was that Howard Hughes was the silent partner with his twenty-five percent share. Then Hepburn waived her salary in favor of a percentage—ten percent of the Broadway gross and slightly more from the road company. She also very shrewdly purchased the movie rights.

On the night of March 28, 1939, when *The Philadelphia Story* premiered at the Shubert Theater on Broadway, Kath-

THE PHILADELPHIA STORY (1940). With Cary Grant

arine Hepburn achieved her greatest triumph on the stage. Her performance as Tracy Lord was acclaimed for its mercurial excitement and dazzling presence. Her profit from this stage venture is estimated at about half a million dollars.

The second Hollywood coming of Katharine Hepburn took place in June, 1940, before the start of the road tour of *The Philadelphia Story*. She bore the same independent air, but this time, she was much wiser. She was with MGM, the Tiffany of Hollywood studios. She would also have script approval for the first time in her career.

Louis B. Mayer, who wanted to bring the Philip Barry comedy to the screen, was obliged to listen to Hepburn and negotiate on her terms. He paid $250,000 for the film rights, with the actress' services (for a one-picture deal only) as the leading lady. Further, he agreed to get George

Cukor to direct and Cary Grant (with whom Hepburn had made her previous two films) to play C. K. Dexter Haven, the ex-husband intent on keeping Tracy Lord from remarrying. Grant by this time was commanding the top billing which he retained for the remainder of his film career, and, at his insistence, he received it in *The Philadelphia Story*.

In her previous teamings with Grant, Hepburn had been billed first, both in *Bringing Up Baby* and in *Holiday*. Her name had been alone above the title in *Sylvia Scarlett*. Unlike many stars (with Grant the prime example), Katharine Hepburn has remained flexible in her billing over the years, acquiescing to her leading man—Tracy, Bogart, Lancaster, Hope. It was Tracy who allegedly made the statement to Garson Kanin in reply to the suggestion that the lady be billed first in the early Tracy-Hepburn teamings: "This is a movie, chowderhead, not a lifeboat."

Since only eight weeks were available before *The Philadelphia Story* was to begin its national tour, George Cukor had a fairly tight schedule to maintain in filming, and he shot it with virtually no retakes. The screenplay was by Donald Ogden Stewart, who, according to the director, added several original scenes in the style of his good friend Philip Barry, to focus on Hepburn's unique personality. Stewart, it is said, did much the same in his screenplay for *Holiday*.

Every movement, every word, every reaction in *The Philadelphia Story* (1940) was tailored for the actress—since, of course, Philip Barry had seen only Hepburn as Tracy Lord from the instant he had begun to construct the first scene. And the first scene in the film, with Dexter Haven being thrown out of the Lord mansion by Tracy, followed closely by his golf clubs and then by Tracy herself—in a rage—breaking one of the clubs over her knee, marks a delicious prologue to this classic urbane comedy about the mainline Philadelphia "aristocracy." Dexter, in that opening sequence, immediately rises to the occasion and flattens her with one push. Cukor later admitted that the entire scene was an afterthought. "We realized we needed something to reconstruct their marriage, and we didn't want to do it with a lot of dialogue." So he used none.

Tracy is pictured as arrogant, scornful, rapacious. She is so haughty that even the rain

THE PHILADELPHIA STORY (1940). With Cary Grant, James Stewart and Ruth Hussey

wouldn't dare fall on her wedding day because, as her young sister Dinah (played by Virginia Weidler) says: "Tracy wouldn't stand for it." When she has to be, Tracy is also witty, entrancing, mischievous. She is the victim of her whims. The film moves into high gear on the eve of her marriage to stuffy, self-made executive George Kittredge (John Howard)—first, with the return to the Lord household of first husband Dexter Haven, and then with the visit of magazine reporter Mike Connor (James Stewart) and his photographer Liz Imbrie (Ruth Hussey). Both ex-husband Dexter and reporter Mike try to defrost Tracy and, at the same time, dissuade her from taking the imminent trip to the altar.

She tells her ex-husband icily: "You can go right back where you came from." At the same time, she tries to refrain from falling in love with the reporter. To Dexter, she has always been "a virgin goddess"; to Mike, she is "a radiant, glorious queen"; to her father (John Halliday), "a perennial spinster" (shades of later roles) who has "everything it takes to make a lovely woman except the one essential thing—an understanding heart."

Tracy's transformation in *The Philadelphia Story* is from a cold, high-handed snob into a lovely, loving woman. Among the film's highlights is the party scene in which Tracy and Mike get drunk and decide upon a midnight swim in her pool. Mike lovingly whispers to her: "There's a magnificence in you, Tracy. You're lit from within. You're the golden girl, full of life and warmth and delight!"

Both ex-husband Dexter and future-husband George come upon the bathrobed Mike carrying Tracy, who is quite drunk and also wearing a robe. Dexter knocks Mike out before George can. Struggling with a morning-after hangover, Tracy wonders how far things had progressed the night before, and becomes a warmer woman in her frailty. And learning that Mike simply left her on the bed and tiptoed out, she asks him: "Why? Was I so unattractive?" The field of admirers narrows when George finds himself unable to forgive her for humiliating him. Wedding plans progress inexorably with Dexter and Mike both offering to assume the groom's role. Dexter wins a now-radiant Tracy.

In its cover story, *Life* magazine commented: "When Katharine Hepburn sets out to play

THE PHILADELPHIA STORY (1940). With James Stewart

THE PHILADELPHIA STORY (1940). With James Stewart

Katharine Hepburn, she is a sight to behold. Nobody is her equal." The film opened at New York's Radio City Music Hall (her fifteenth in succession) on the day after Christmas, 1940, and became the first picture ever to be held over at that house for more than five weeks. One week after its premiere, Hepburn was selected as the year's Best Actress by the New York Film Critics. She accepted the award over a two-way radio connection from Dallas, where she was appearing in the national company of the play. As part of the ceremonies, Hepburn did a brief scene from the play.

She was also nominated for her third Academy Award, but lost to Ginger Rogers for *Kitty Foyle.* Cukor received a nomination for his direction, Ruth Hussey for Best Supporting Actress, and the film itself for Best Picture. James Stewart won his only Oscar (to date) as Best Actor and Donald Ogden Stewart won his for the screenplay.

For the record, the stage version of *The Philadelphia Story* featured, in addition to Hepburn, Joseph Cotten as Dexter, Van Heflin as Mike (a part written especially for him by Barry at Hepburn's request), and Shirley Booth as Liz. In *High Society,* the 1956 musical remake, with one of Cole Porter's last film scores, Grace Kelly was Tracy, Bing Crosby was Dexter, Frank Sinatra was Mike, and Celeste Holm was Liz.

Interestingly, announcement was made in 1968 of a musical version of Philip Barry's *Holiday* for Broadway, with a score comprised of unpublished Cole Porter songs, but the production never materialized.

After completing the film version of *The Philadelphia Story,* Hepburn toured the country with the play, closing finally in Philadelphia in February, 1941. Her only film work that year:

speaking the narration (written by Eleanor Roosevelt) for a documentary short entitled *Women in Defense.*

Shortly after finishing her tour with the Barry comedy, Hepburn was approached, at Garson Kanin's suggestion, by Ring Lardner Jr. and Michael Kanin (Garson's brother). They had concocted a screenplay about a down-to-earth sportswriter and a sophisticated columnist, both working for the same newspaper and feuding with each other in their separate columns. They finally meet, fall in love, marry—and continue feuding.

Hepburn took it upon herself to assume the off-screen role of writers' agent, and she sent the script to Louis B. Mayer—after removing the names of Lardner and Kanin. Mayer, favorably impressed by this "anonymous" script, forwarded it to his producer, Joseph L. Mankiewicz, who previously had done *The Philadelphia Story.* The latter was said to have concluded that the authors were Ben Hecht and Charles MacArthur, who, because of prior commitments elsewhere, had chosen not to put their names on the screenplay, which was entitled *Woman of the Year.*

Then, as he had had to do once before, Louis B. Mayer was obliged to discuss terms with Miss Hepburn. Her price tag for the property: $211,000. The breakdown of figures: $100,000 for her salary as star, $10,000 as her agent's fee, $1,000 in moving expenses to the west coast, and $100,000 for the anonymous scenarists.

L. B. Mayer acceded to all her demands including co-star and director approval. He finally concluded that it might be to his advantage to sign Katharine Hepburn to a long-term star contract rather than face this periodic haggling whenever she brought him interesting film properties.

Hepburn requested George Cukor as her director, but he was working with Garbo, so she asked for George Stevens, whose services Mayer secured from Columbia Pictures. For her leading man, she wanted Spencer Tracy, whom the sports columnist in the story resembled more than casually. Among the reasons: Garson Kanin had long been a friend, separately, of both Hepburn and Tracy, and Ring Lardner Jr. was the son of one of Tracy's Lambs Club buddies. Mayer was unable to deliver Tracy, who was then on location in Florida with Ann Harding, filming *The Yearling.*

WOMAN OF THE YEAR (1942). With Spencer Tracy

WOMAN OF THE YEAR (1942). With Spencer Tracy

WOMAN OF THE YEAR (1942). With Spencer Tracy and William Bendix

As other choices for the leading man were being submitted to Hepburn, *The Yearling* company, encountering difficulties, suddenly suspended shooting. MGM finally scrapped the project, and revived it later with Gregory Peck and Jane Wyman as the stars. Spencer Tracy became available, and the memorable comedy called *Woman of the Year* began production. The famous account of the initial Tracy - Hepburn face - to - face meeting (allegedly, each had been screening the other's films secretly for weeks) often has been repeated. The dialogue, however, is usually attributed to the wrong party. To Hepburn's comment,

"I'm afraid I'm a bit tall for Mr. Tracy," it was producer Mankiewicz—and not Tracy—who replied: "Don't worry, he'll cut you down to size."

Woman of the Year launched one of the most popular and certainly one of the most felicitous starring combinations in screen history, performing together in nine films over the next quarter century. So well did they complement one another that, during the run of her MGM contract, only their movies together were successes (with the possible exception of Tracy's *Father of the Bride*).

As the competitive, totally mismatched columnists who are

given to thrashing out the comparative importance of their jobs, the two artists were in fine fettle, working in perfect counterpoint as though they had spent their entire individual careers perfecting this professional relationship. Hepburn, as columnist Tess Harding, said to be patterned after Dorothy Thompson mixed with a dash of Claire Booth Luce, "is just right," noted *Time* magazine in its review of the film. "For once, strident Katharine Hepburn is properly subdued." Tracy's Sam Craig is everybody's conception of how a sports editor should look and sound. Whether as battling journalists or, later, man and wife, both are fiercely independent. He calls her "the Calamity Jane of the fast International Set"; she refers to him as "an ostrich with amnesia."

To get their strange love affair off the ground, Sam tries to introduce Tess to baseball, vainly explaining the game's fine points to her. Stressing that a good pitch must pass between the batter's shoulders and knees, Sam is dismayed when Tess suggests: "If the batter were smart, he'd stoop down and fool the pitcher."

The film has many other highlights: Sam's unintentional intrusion on a crowded women's meeting while searching for Tess; his total ineptness at proposing and her total ineptness at making her first wifely breakfast; Sam's bender when Tess insists on pursuing her career and is named "Woman of the Year"; Tess' disastrous attempts at writing Sam's sports column while he's off getting drunk; and her even more disastrous efforts at domesticity when she wants to be reconciled with him. (Working at besting the kitchen appliances at their own sneaky game, she ends up with misbehaving eggs, overboiling coffee, alarmingly yeasty waffles, and toast that pops up frenetically.)

In addition to introducing Tracy and Hepburn as a team, *Women of the Year* marked the screen debut of William Bendix as a bartender who once fought Jim Braddock. Others in support were Fay Bainter as Tess' crusading aunt, Minor Watson as her father, Reginald Owen as her editor, and Dan Tobin as her officious secretary.

Filming was done between late July and mid-October of 1941 and MGM considered rushing it into release for Academy Award contention. It was held back, however, until early the following year. Hepburn received her fourth Oscar nomination for Tess Harding, losing out to

KEEPER OF THE FLAME (1942). With Spencer Tracy

KEEPER OF THE FLAME (1942). With Spencer Tracy and Darryl Hickman

KEEPER OF THE FLAME (1942). With Spencer Tracy

Greer Garson's Kay Miniver. For their original screenplay, Ring Lardner Jr. and Michael Kanin won Academy Awards. Tracy and Hepburn recreated their roles as Sam and Tess in a thirty-minute radio version of *Woman of the Year* on the Screen Guild Theater in the spring of 1943. It was their only appearance together outside of films.

Shortly after *Woman of the Year* premiered, Hepburn once again returned to the stage, opposite Elliott Nugent in *Without Love,* another comedy written especially for her by Phi-

lip Barry. She opened in Princeton, New Jersey, on March 5, 1942, and toured for two months. Then Barry decided that the show needed to be rewritten, and the Broadway opening was deferred until the fall. Hepburn went back to Hollywood.

The outstanding success of *Woman of the Year* and the chemistry of its two stars was not lost on Louis B. Mayer, who decided to tempt fate by experimenting with the Tracy-Hepburn combination in drama. Mayer assigned George Cukor to direct the pair in Donald Ogden Stewart's adaptation of I.A.R.

Wylie's suspense novel, *Keeper of the Flame.* Hepburn was cast as the widow of eminent American Robert Forrest, who tries to prevent a noted journalist (Tracy) from discovering that her husband had been a Fascist. This melodramatic exercise in patriotism was in marked contrast to the sophisticated entertainment provided by *Woman of the Year* which had preceded it and, except for *The Sea of Grass,* all of the Tracy-Hepburn films which were to follow.

Keeper of the Flame (1942) was unusual primarily for the total absence of any romantic interest between the two stars. It was simply a slow-moving one-hundred minutes showing a reporter trying to get a story and a wealthy woman trying to keep a secret. At the finale, she breaks down after being confronted with documentation, and confesses her husband's activities, and is shot by the dead man's confidential secretary (Richard Whorf), who puts a torch to the house. The reporter tries desperately to save her, but, as she dies, she whispers to him: "Write your story. Don't spare Robert. Don't spare me." And in the finest tradition of high-gloss soap opera, Tracy thrusts aside his sorrow and plunges into the task of writing the true story of the man America had come to revere.

Hepburn had been involving herself more deeply in films in recent years and never hesitated to offer suggestions to her directors and to her fellow performers. It is said that she knew not only her own lines but everybody else's, before the cameras began to roll. During the filming of *Keeper of the Flame,* she confided to Cukor after he had shot a scene, "I don't think that was done correctly. I think Spencer should have been sitting when he spoke his lines." Cukor remained silent. Later she told him: "Christine should speak those lines more softly. It wasn't done correctly." Still no response from the director. Still later, after Cukor had filmed a fire scene, she spoke up again. "I don't think they would have to be told about the fire. They would smell the smoke." Cukor finally broke his silence. "It must be wonderful to know all about acting *and* all about fires."

The excellent supporting cast included Margaret Wycherly (whose son Anthony Veiller coauthored the screenplays for Hepburn's *Break of Hearts, A Woman Rebels,* and *Stage Door*) playing Hepburn's mother-in-law, Forrest Tucker as her cousin, Donald Meek as a hotel desk clerk, Horace (later Stephen)

DRAGON SEED (1944). As Jade

McNally and Audrey Christie as two of Tracy's newspaper friends, and Percy Kilbride, as a taxi driver.

Everything about the production—from Adrian's gowns to William Daniels' photography to Bronislau Kaper's score—was top drawer. And it was Hepburn's last romantic glamour girl role. Yet ultimately the film was nothing more than a turgid melodrama disguised as a psychological thriller with a sociological message.

By the time shooting was completed for *Keeper of the Flame*, Philip Barry had rewritten his latest comedy of manners, *Without Love*, to his and Hepburn's satisfaction, and the actress made her last trip of the decade back to the stage. A two-week tryout began in Detroit on October 26, 1942, prior to moving on to Broadway. The Hepburn commitment was for a sixteen-week run—through February 13, 1943. While performing in New York in *Without Love*, the star lent her talents, along with sixty-five others from the Lunts and Katharine Cornell (in rare screen appearances) to Harpo Marx, Johnny Weissmuller, and Ed Wynn, to *Stage Door Canteen* (1943). The film was a patriotic tribute to the popular canteens of World War II which were operated for visiting servicemen in a number of major cities by the American Theatre Wing.

An odd choice for Katharine Hepburn's next movie project was the massive film version of Pearl S. Buck's *Dragon Seed* (1944). MGM hoped to duplicate the success and the prestige of its excellent film production of another story by Miss Buck, *The Good Earth.* A large, heterogeneous cast was put through its paces by two of MGM's minor directors, Jack Conway and Harold S. Bucquet, to relate the lengthy story of a Chinese girl who thirsts for knowledge in books and, realizing that without freedom her nation cannot be strong, becomes a dynamic leader in the fight against Japanese oppression.

Dragon Seed, photographed in the San Fernando Valley by Sidney Wagner (who received an Oscar nomination for his work), found Hepburn as the idealistic Jade, peasant girl-turned-guerilla fighter. Her sharp Anglo-Saxon features were softened as much as makeup artist Jack Dawn and his staff could manage; her high-necked, tufted-cotton outfits were as authentically Chinese as Irene could recreate. Hepburn spoke at the time of her apprehensions

DRAGON SEED (1944). With Turhan Bey

about her many monologues in the film: "Somebody is certainly going to say I can't keep still, even in Chinese."

Naturally, the critics were divided in their appraisals both of the film and of the characterizations. *Time* called the movie "a kind of slant-eyed *North Star.*" The *New York Times'* Paul P. Kennedy found Hepburn "brittle and unresilient throughout, and constantly betrayed by an accent she has made into her trademark of sophisticated drama." Archer Winsten said in the *New York Post:* "Katharine Hepburn's memorable timbre defies all efforts at disguise."

Among the noted "Oriental" types in the cast of *Dragon Seed* were Walter Huston, virtually

71

DRAGON SEED (1944). With Aline MacMahon, Walter Huston and Turhan Bey

repeating his *North Star* role in a Chinese peasant's outfit, Aline MacMahon as his wife (her believable interpretation won her an Academy Award nomination), Turhan Bey (on loan from Maria Montez and Universal) in the single first-rate role of his career, Agnes Moorehead, J. Carrol Naish, newcomer Hurd Hatfield, and, as the Chinese quisling, Akim Tamiroff, "whose speech," noted the *New York Times,* "falls upon the ear as resonantly as the sound of a gefülte fish banged against a temple gong."

Several of Hollywood's standard Orientals, including Philip Ahn and Benson Fong, were gratuitously thrown into the fray. Lionel Barrymore spoke the offscreen narration and filled in

gaps in the continuity. The film came to a crashing finale, just prior to the then-obligatory patriotic sentiments, with Hepburn preparing a ceremonial banquet for the invaders from the East with a generous amount of poison, thus wiping out the entire Japanese command for her region of China.

Dragon Seed might have sidetracked her career temporarily, but the film version of *Without Love* (1945) placed the actress once again back on the main line. The movie of the Barry comedy surpassed the stage version, and it reunited the Tracy-Hepburn team. Donald Ogden Stewart was called upon to do another of his superlative adaptations, and in the process he made a number of changes in the transformation from stage to screen. In the play, the leading lady proposes a platonic marriage to a young diplomat with whom she has been living for several months. He will accept a marriage "without love" because of an unhappy affair in the past; she prefers a marriage "without love" because her husband's death destroyed her one and only perfect marriage.

On film she's a widow with a large house in wartime Washington, and he's an inventor seeking a place to hang his hat and conduct his secret experiments for the government. Since this was the era of highly moral films—in the interest of patriotism and sundry national causes —any intimation of extra-marital hanky-panky was studiously avoided. Hepburn gives Tracy the run of the house while she lives out on her farm. The idea of a platonic marriage arises from his need for an assistant and her wish to help the war effort.

Naturally, all manner of intimate and embarrassing situations arise—when they are forced to share a compartment on a train, Tracy insists that Hepburn tie him into the upper berth—but they manage to carry on "without love" until the final reel.

The New Yorker loved *Without Love* and decided: "Miss Hepburn and Mr. Tracy

WITHOUT LOVE (1945). With Spencer Tracy

WITHOUT LOVE (1945). With Spencer Tracy

WITHOUT LOVE (1945). With Spencer Tracy

succeed brilliantly in the leading parts. The somewhat metallic and stylized quality of Miss Hepburn's acting is almost perfectly suited to a role that is largely a vehicle for fashionable humor." And the *Time* review said: "Miss Hepburn, whose Bryn Mawr drawl and tailored walk sometimes gets in her way, brings this sort of lady to life more convincingly than could anybody else in pictures."

This witty, glossy comedy was competently handled by Harold S. Bucquet, one of the co-directors of *Dragon Seed,* and boasted the sparkling photography of ace cameraman Karl Freund. Lucille Ball, a wise-cracking Broadway ingenue in Hepburn's *Stage Door,* played a wise-cracking real estate agent in *Without Love.* Director Bucquet later made this comment about the Tracy-Hepburn combination: "Miss Hepburn requires direction, for she tends to act too much. Her acting is much less economical than Mr. Tracy's, but his style is rubbing off on her. The important thing is that I don't coach them on their scenes together. No one should do that, for they do a thorough job by themselves and know exactly what they want to accomplish when we begin a scene."

THE SEA OF GRASS (1947).
With Spencer Tracy

More more than a year after *Without Love,* Hepburn was away from movie-making. Tracy had gone east to star on Broadway in Robert E. Sherwood's *The Rugged Path,* directed by Garson Kanin. The play, Tracy's last, closed after its eighty-first performance. MGM awaited his return in order to reunite its premier screen team. Elia Kazan's rambling film version of Conrad Richter's novel, *The Sea of Grass* (1947), was the chosen vehicle.

When Tracy made his reappearance on the MGM lot, he sported a new image—his hair had turned gray, giving him an appearance that widened the age differential between him and

THE SEA OF GRASS (1947).
With Spencer Tracy

Hepburn. In the case of *The Sea of Grass,* the new image was just right. Kazan, working on only his second major film, immediately began to clash with Tracy, and it became Katharine Hepburn's major responsibility throughout the production to arbitrate their disputes and prevent them from coming to blows. Kazan's introspective, psychological, fussy, Actors' Studio approach was diametrically opposed to Tracy's craft-oriented, instinctive style of acting, and the seventy-five day shooting schedule was filled with tensions.

The director recently admitted that, contrary to the reams of MGM publicity about the rigors of location-shooting and the hardships encountered by the high-priced cast, the entire film was shot in front of a rear-projection screen, with the actors and two or three live horses strategically placed. He also said that he hated the film, but made this comment of his leading lady: "I was very proud I got Katharine Hepburn to cry, because I thought she was a cool person. Not at all—if she wants to cry, she turns it on." He recalled getting into a hassle with Louis B. Mayer because of Hepburn's crying style, and he quoted Mayer as saying: "Some people cry with their voice, some with their nose, some with their throat, some with their eyes. But she cries with everything! And this is excessive!"

Primarily because of a poor script by Marguerite Roberts and Vincent Lawrence, the resulting film was a boring, actionless western drama about a cattle baron whose obsession with his landed domain causes his wife to leave him for an affair with his bitter enemy, gloomily played by Melvyn Douglas. In its advertising campaign, MGM tried to generate interest by stressing the action and sex angles: "Rugged TRACY (he lived as ruthlessly as he ruled)! Romantic HEPBURN (her indiscretion cost a lifetime of happiness)! Reckless WALKER (he

UNDERCURRENT (1946). With Robert Taylor

was born without a name and became a killer)! Ruthless DOUGLAS (he was the schemer who loved unwisely)!" Interestingly, Hepburn's illegitimate son in *The Sea of Grass* was Robert Walker, who was to play her lover in their next film together.

As Lutie Cameron Brewton, Hepburn gave another of her independent woman characterizations, with the Old West as a backdrop. Lutie's idea of expressing herself strongly is to sleep with her husband's mortal enemy while her husband is dutifully tending the Back Forty of his king-sized ranch. After over two hours of this, the wronged husband and the errant wife de-

cide, for the sake of their now-grown daughter (Phyllis Thaxter) and because of the shooting of the villainous bastard son, to reunite and to grow old together.

The Sea of Grass was shot, edited and then shelved until early 1947. When Bosley Crowther finally reviewed it in the *New York Times*, he wrote: "Miss Hepburn's performance as Tracy's helpmate is so rigidly attitudinized that her scenes, either alone or with others, are distressingly pompous and false."

Immediately after finishing *The Sea of Grass*, Hepburn was given the lead in *Undercurrent*

UNDERCURRENT (1946).
As Ann Hamilton

(1946) opposite Robert Taylor who had just returned from wartime duty. The screenplay was fashioned by Edward Chodorov from a short story entitled *You Were There* by Thelma Stradel, published in *Women's Home Companion*. It is curious that MGM would welcome back its dynamic, dashing star with a role requiring him to be dour and malevolent—and to act in such a lurid melodrama. The directing assignment went to Vincente Minnelli (his seventh film), whose forte was musicals. He was helped immensely by cinematographer Karl Freund, who kept all of the suspense-heightening shadows in the right places. Although MGM exhorted in its ad campaign, "Please don't tell the terrific ending!" it became evident early in the film sequences who was doing what to whom.

Hepburn played the rather dowdy, small-town daughter of a noted scientist (Edmund Gwenn). Swept off her feet by wealthy industrialist Taylor, she marries him and finds herself outclassed socially. While worrying about improving her wardrobe and learning how to hold her own in conversation with her husband's friends, she stumbles upon a family secret involving Taylor's mysterious half-brother (Robert Mitchum). Her curiosity causes her husband to unmask himself as a vicious psychopath.

Although the *New Yorker* repeated the standard comment generally expressed by one critic or another about nearly every performance by the actress— "Katharine Hepburn employs all her celebrated mannerisms" —Hepburn won good personal reviews as the shy young girl-cum - smartly - tailored sophisticate. (Irene had created a lovely wardrobe for her). *Undercurrent* had its New York premiere in late November, 1946, and marked the first Hepburn film in thirteen years (discounting *Stage Door Canteen*) which was not featured at Radio City Music Hall. *The Sea of Grass* followed *Undercurrent* into release by less than three months. Between filming those two productions, the actress made an appearance in David O. Selznick's all-star *The American Creed*, a patriotic trailer to promote American Brotherhood Week. She and Spencer Tracy also narrated a short film for the American Cancer Society.

Just as MGM had announced in early 1946 that Hepburn would star in the film version of the Elizabeth Goudge novel *Green Dolphin Street*, the studio promised early the following year that the public would see her in its production of J. P. Marquand's *B. F.'s Daughter*. Had she starred in either, she would have once again acted opposite Van Heflin. Instead, she was given *Song of Love* (1947), a glossy black-and-white soap opera with music, adapted from an obscure play about Robert and Clara Schumann. Hepburn gave an interesting interpretation of Clara Wieck, the famed concert pianist who married composer Robert Schumann and had an affair with his pupil, Johannes Brahms. The film was produced and directed with all the finest trappings by Clarence Brown and toiled over by no less than four screenwriters.

The movie was prefaced by

SONG OF LOVE (1947). With Paul Henreid

the admission that "certain liberties" had been taken with biographical facts—such as turning Clara Wieck Schumann into a glamorized (costumes by Irene) hausfrau. As a "pianist," however, Hepburn was totally believable, thanks to weeks of training in the fundamentals of the piano. Artur Rubinstein provided the off-screen renditions by Schumann, Brahms, and Liszt. Of the actress' performance, *Time* said: "Clara Schumann, one of the great women of her century, was presumably free from Katharine Hepburn's narrow, rather collegiate type of jitters. But Miss Hepburn portrays Clara with skill and feeling. She is fascinating to watch at the piano,

SONG OF LOVE (1947). With Robert Walker

SONG OF LOVE (1947). With Robert Walker and Paul Henreid

using the clawlike eighteenth-century style; her 'reactions' to the men's music, in various dramatic contexts, are the backbone of the picture."
texts, are the backbone of the picture."

Critic Jack Moffitt, writing in *Esquire,* found: "When Miss Hepburn gets a real part, she knows what to do with it. In *Song of Love* the accent is on acting. Katie stops playing Katharine Hepburn and becomes Clara Wieck with a skill that places her in the first rank among screen performers." Apparently her performances in *The Philadelphia Story* and *Woman of the Year,* as well as *Little Women* and *Alice Adams,* eluded that critic.

On the other hand, Bosley Crowther, writing in the *New York Times,* thought the Hepburn performance was "one of her familiarly agonized jobs—a compound of soulful expressions, fluttered hands and prideful lifts of the head." One bit of dialogue in an early portion of *Song of Love* was a variation on Menjou's statement to Hepburn in *Morning Glory:* "You don't belong to any man now; you belong to Broadway." As Clara, Hepburn defiantly goes over the head of her father (Leo G. Carroll), taking into the courts her

plea for permission to marry Schumann (Paul Henreid). The judge tells her: "I dispose not only of your heart, but of something else that hardly belongs to you—your talent. It belongs to the world."

In *Song of Love,* Johannes Brahms was played by Robert Walker, who, less than a year earlier, had portrayed Jerome Kern in *Till the Clouds Roll By.* Somewhere in the back of L. B. Mayer's mind had probably been etched what was thought to be a remarkable likeness between the two composers. In any event, Walker was as wrong as Brahms as he had been as Kern. And of Henry Daniell's conception of Franz Liszt in *Song of Love,* the *New York Times* had this stinging comment: "(It is) reminiscent of the Phantom of the Opera on a night out."

The next year, *State of the Union* (1948) reunited Hepburn with Spencer Tracy almost by accident and became the last of twenty-two Hepburn films to premiere at Radio City Music Hall. Her participation with the property goes back to its very origins. Howard Lindsay and Russel Crouse wrote *State of the Union* in the mid-forties with Helen Hayes in mind for the role of Mary Matthews, wife of the Republican candidate for Pres-

STATE OF THE UNION (1948).
With Spencer Tracy

ident of the United States. Miss Hayes turned it down, as did both Margaret Sullavan and Katharine Hepburn. The part subsequently went to Ruth Hussey who starred opposite Ralph Bellamy, and the play went on to win the Pulitzer Prize.

Movie rights were purchased by Liberty Films, an independent company which had been formed by Frank Capra, William Wyler, George Stevens, and Samuel Briskin. An initial nine-picture deal had been negotiated with RKO Pictures, which provided for three productions each from Capra, Wyler, and Stevens. It's A Wonderful Life was the first venture under the deal; State of the Union was to be the second. RKO, however, balked at the latter's budget of $2,800,000.

Since Spencer Tracy had expressed a desire to do the film, a deal was then struck with Louis B. Mayer, similar to the one which brought Gone with the Wind under MGM's distribution banner. Tracy would be loaned to Liberty Films in exchange for MGM's releasing rights. Claudette Colbert was then signed for the female lead. On the very eve of production, Miss Colbert brought to director Capra's attention the fact that her customary five-o'clock-stop clause was missing from the contract. Hasty negotiations got nowhere and the actress walked out.

In his book, The Name Above the Title, Frank Capra discusses a call he placed to Tracy, who suggested that Katharine Hepburn might be interested in the part. Said the actor: "The bag of bones has been helping me rehearse. Kinda stops you, Frank, the way she reads the woman's part. She's a real theater nut, you know. She might do it for the hell of it."

The director went on: "There are women and there are women —and then there is Katie. There are actresses and actresses— then there is Hepburn. A rare professional-amateur, acting is her hobby, her living, her love." He later noted: "When Tracy and his 'bag of bones' played a

STATE OF THE UNION (1948). With Van Johnson, Irving Bacon, Angela Lansbury, and Adolphe Menjou

scene, cameras, lights, microphones, and written scripts ceased to exist. And the director did just what the crews and other actors did—sat, watched, and marveled."

State of the Union was fashioned from the Lindsay-Crouse play by Anthony Veiller and Myles Connolly and featured high-powered performers in support of Tracy as the liberal-minded tycoon who is offered the Republican nomination and Hepburn as his estranged wife who stays by his side for propriety's sake. Cast members included Van Johnson as a Drew Pearson-type columnist, Angela Lansbury as the newspaper publisher's daughter who craves power and becomes Tracy's mistress, Adolphe Menjou (acting with Hepburn for the third time) as a conniving, old-line

politico, and Lewis Stone as Lansbury's father.

The announcement that Hepburn had been signed to costar in *State of the Union* brought protests from various quarters on grounds of her "Red leanings"—i.e., her support of Henry Wallace and her defense of him in 1947 when he was accused of being a pawn for the Communists. During the House Un-American Activities Committee (HUAC) inquiry into the motion picture industry in the late forties, Hepburn gave her only known political speech, lambasting the "smear campaign" of J. Parnell Thomas, the committee's chairman. She said, in part: "The artist since the beginning of time has always expressed the aspirations and dreams of his people. Silence the artist and you have silenced the most articulate voice the people have." Adolphe Menjou's activities at that time, especially his exuberant cooperation with HUAC's Hollywood witch-hunt, did nothing to endear him to his friend, Katharine Hepburn, and from that time forward, their speaking relationship was limited to the scenes they had together in *State of the Union.*

The film premiered at the Capitol Theater in Washington D.C. in May, 1948, at a gala black-tie affair with President Harry S Truman and his daughter, Margaret, in attendance. Tracy and Hepburn were not.

Howard Barnes, writing in the *New York Herald-Tribune,* said of Hepburn's performance: "She is restrained, persuasive and altogether delightful." Bosley Crowther thought she "gives every assurance of making the most stylish First Lady we've had in years." An interesting sidelight: *State of the Union* today appears on television sporting the Paramount logo instead of Leo the Lion preceding the opening credits, due to a complicated packaging transaction.

Following *State of the Union,* Capra had hoped to make *Woman of Distinction* with Katharine Hepburn and Ray Milland, either for MGM where

ADAM'S RIB (1949). With Spencer Tracy

she was working, or for Paramount where the actor was under contract. Whatever deals and counter-deals ensued, the director ended up remaking his own *Broadway Bill* (as *Riding High* with Bing Crosby), Milland went to Columbia to star opposite Rosalind Russell in *Woman of Distinction* (which Capra had sold), and Hepburn was to have gotten the role of the alcoholic wife opposite Tracy in *Edward My Son,* which Cukor was to shoot in England from Donald Ogden Stewart's screenplay. Instead, the role went to Deborah Kerr, but Hepburn accompanied the crew to England, remained for the entire shooting schedule and was not seen again on the screen for more than sixteen months.

ADAM'S RIB (1949). With Tom Ewell

ADAM'S RIB (1949). With Marvin Kaplan, Clarence Kolb and Judy Holliday

ADAM'S RIB (1949). With Spencer Tracy, David Wayne and Judy Holliday

During that time, changes were being made at MGM. The Supreme Court had directed Loew's (MGM) to divest itself of its theatres—and also applied the ruling to RKO, Warners, Paramount, and 20th Century-Fox. Dore Schary had become installed as executive in charge of production at MGM, forecasting the imminent change in command and the gradual easing out of Louis B. Mayer.

Tracy and Hepburn were reunited at MGM early in 1949, for more saucy husband-wife rivalry in *Adam's Rib*. The story was written especially for them by their close friends, Ruth Gordon and Garson Kanin, and in the director's chair was George Cukor. As a married couple as well as opposing lawyers, Tracy and Hepburn starred in one of the year's brightest, most literate, and most successful films.

Around the simple framework of the trial of a woman charged with shooting her husband whom she had found in the arms of another woman, the Kanins constructed an hilarious comedy about two intelligent professionals, proud of each other's courtroom accomplishments and above all, happily married. They are not, however, above continuing the ages-old war between the sexes. This particular case finds Adam and Amanda Bonner (in private, "Pinky" and "Pinkie") pitted against one another across the counsel's table in court. He's the prosecuting attorney while she represents the wronged wife. She finds the courtroom the perfect soapbox for her theories about women's rights, arguing somewhat illogically but delightfully that a man would not be prosecuted for shooting an unfaithful wife, therefore no double standard should be applied.

Take, for instance, Hepburn's summation to the jury: "An unwritten law stands back of a man who fights to defend his home. Apply the same to this maltreated wife and neglected mother. We ask no more. Equality! Deep in the interior of South America, there thrives a civilization, far older than ours, a people known as the Lorcananos, descended from the Amazons. In this vast tribe, members of the female sex rule and govern and systematically deny equal rights to the men—made weak and puny by years of subservience. Too weak to revolt. And yet how long have we lived in the shadow of a like injustice?"

Previous to this emasculating speech, she has used the entire trial to publicly embarrass her husband, encouraging one witness, a female weightlifter (hilariously played by Hope Emerson), to demonstrate, with lawyer Tracy as substitute, her proficiency with barbells. Tracy angrily looks down toward the bench to register his strong objections. Other choice moments include the intimate Tracy-Hepburn tete-a-tetes under the counsels' table, with each private "conference" being signalled by Tracy conveniently

dropping his pencil to the floor; Tracy's knockdown fight with next-door neighbor and lothario songwriter David Wayne who has been pursuing Hepburn for years, and Tracy's final tactic to bring Hepburn into line by using her own most reliable trick: tears —large, pathetic tears rolling down his cheeks.

"All right, then," she asks him. "What have you proved? What does that show?" "Shows the score," he replies. She: "Shows what I say is true; no difference between the sexes. None. Men, women, the same." He: "They are, huh?" She: "Well, maybe there *is* a difference. But it's a *little* difference." He: "Yuh, well as the French say." She: "How do they say?" He: "Vive la difference!" She: "Which means?" He: "Which means hurray for that little difference!"

Three actors received big boosts through their prominent roles in *Adam's Rib:* Judy Holliday (who had worked briefly with Cukor in *Winged Victory*), David Wayne, and Tom Ewell, all from the Broadway stage. Through her classic dumb blonde performance as the wife accused of pulling the trigger, Judy Holliday was launched on a major screen career. David Wayne was the songwriter who "composed" for Hepburn the tune *Farewell Amanda,* written for the film by Cole Porter and heard throughout. Tom Ewell played the target of Miss Holliday's misguided aim.

Besides the scripted antics of the film, an unwritten but carefully planned conspiracy was unfolding behind the cameras. The secret plot, hatched by Hepburn, Kanin, and Cukor, was to secure for Judy Holliday the starring role (which she had created on the stage) in the film version of Kanin's *Born Yesterday,* which Cukor was to direct next for Columbia. Harry Cohn had to be convinced it would be an error in judgment to give the part of Billie Dawn on the screen to anyone but Miss Holliday. Thus, the Holliday role in *Adam's Rib* was purposely built up, and Hepburn threw more than one scene her way. Tom Ewell later disclosed that Hepburn had insisted that Judy Holliday dominate all of their scenes together and then she made certain that none of the younger actress's scenes were tampered with in the editing room. This generous gesture would have astounded those of the Hollywood community who recalled Hepburn as being temperamental, rude, and insensitive during her first decade in their midst. Her second decade was marked by a change to graciousness, affability, and tact.

Adam's Rib was MGM's big Christmas 1949 attraction and won for Ruth Gordon and Garson Kanin an Oscar nomination for Best Original Screenplay. In 1949, Hepburn was seen once again in a scene from *The Philadelphia Story* as well as in one from *Adam's Rib,* both incorporated into a forty-minute trailer entitled *Some of the Best,* an assemblage of clips celebrating MGM's Silver Anniversary. These were scenes from two dozen of what the front office considered the studio's best films from the past and from eighteen movies MGM was releasing in 1949. Lionel Barrymore provided the commentary.

The passion to do Shakespeare surfaced again with Hepburn in 1950, and at the end of January, she opened on Broadway as Rosalind in the Theatre Guild's revival of *As You Like It.* Playing Orlando opposite her was William Prince, and in the company were Cloris Leachman as Celia and Jay Robinson, who would later score in films (as Caligula in *The Robe*). Hepburn followed her critically acclaimed Broadway run of 145 performances with a dazzling cross-country tour.

Her subsequent excursions into Shakespeare occupied a good deal of her professional time during the succeeding decade and included a tour of Australia in 1955 with the Old Vic Company and guest appearances in 1957 and 1960 at the American Shakespeare Festival in Stratford, Connecticut.

While performing on the road in *As You Like It,* the actress was approached by John Huston who asked her to appear in the film *The African Queen* which he and James Agee were preparing. Based on C. S. Forester's 1935 novel, it was to be the second production for Horizon Pictures, the company Huston had formed with producer Sam Spiegel who used the name S. P. Eagle. The screenplay was a collaboration between Huston and the former *Time* film critic and focused in a serio-comic way on the relationship between a prim missionary-spinster and a bibulous riverboat skipper in the heart of World War I Africa. (John Mills recently revealed that he had been offered the role of Charlie Allnut to Bette Davis' Rosie Sayer in the late forties, presumably before Huston had acquired the property.)

The African Queen (1951) marked a number of "firsts" for

THE AFRICAN QUEEN (1951).
With Humphrey Bogart

Hepburn. It was her first film in Technicolor and her first ever made away from Hollywood. With Humphrey Bogart as the male lead, Huston had come up with one of the screen's all-time off-beat casting coups. Speculation was rampant on two points: How would Katharine Hepburn take to Africa? How would Humphrey Bogart take to Hepburn?

On the first question: she found Africa, according to Huston, "utterly divine," and the

THE AFRICAN QUEEN (1951). With Humphrey Bogart.

flora and fauna? "So terribly charming." On the second: she was quickly accepted as "one of the boys" after her initial lecture to Bogart and Huston on their drinking habits and their bawdy camaraderie.

"The idea of making *The African Queen* on location," Huston later wrote, "was not based on capturing the African flora and fauna in Technicolor. We wanted to put the accent on the people; the animals had been covered more than adequately in earlier African films. The point about location filming is that if the actors are living in a certain way, it will come out in their performances. Their very hardships give character to the finished film."

In Charlie and Rosie, Bogart and Hepburn had roles which in-

deed rank among the best of their long careers. From their initial meeting when Rosie acts the proper hostess by serving a spot of tea and Charlie tries to divert attention from his rumbling stomach, *The African Queen* remains a total joy. "Just listen to that stomach of mine," Charlie says. "Way it sounds, you'd think I'd got an 'eye-ener inside me." Rosie graciously changes the subject: "Do have another cup of tea, Mr. Allnut." And Charlie indelicately brings it back: "Thanks, Miss, don't mind if I do. Queer thing, ain't it. What I mean is what d'ya s'pose it is, makes a man's stomach carry on like that?"

From this introductory chatter, through their trip together down river to Limbasi as Rosie helps Charlie plot the destruction of a German gunboat blocking their way to freedom, she slowly begins to let her hair down as he just as slowly begins to act more gentlemanly and protective. "Mr. Allnut." "Yes, Miss." "What did you say is in these boxes with the red lines on them?" "That's blastin' gelatine, Miss." "Isn't it dangerous?"

He soon gets the drift of her conversation and realizes he is beginning to lose command of the ship. She asks him: "You're a machinist, aren't you? Wasn't that your position at the mine?" He replies: "Yeah, kind of fixer. Jack of all trades and master of none, like they say." She: "Could you make a torpedo?" He: "Come again, Miss?"

The turning point is reached when he gets roaring drunk and refers to her as "you crazy, psalm-singing, skinny old maid." When he passes out, she pours his entire gin supply overboard and forces a new relationship under a different set of standards. When tempers have cooled after days of frosty silence, love sets in, and they begin to get acquainted. "Dear," she says, "there's something I simply must know . . . what's your first name?" "Charlie," he replies. "Charlie—Charlie—Charlie," she moons. "Give us

THE AFRICAN QUEEN (1951).
As Rose Sayer

another kiss," he urges. "Charlie —Charlie, dear. This must be one of the loveliest places in Africa."

Rosie has now assumed command of the operation with Charlie unwittingly reduced to first mate. Classic sequences from this memorable film include Bogart and Hepburn wading waist deep down the river, she hacking away at the underbrush, he dragging "The African Queen" to more maneuverable waters; Bogart frantically trying to rid himself of the leeches ("Augh, the little buggers—Pull 'em off me, Rosie— Anything I hate in this world it's leeches—filthy devils!"); the destruction of the German cruiser as the two strangely-paired adventurers are about to be hanged on its deck. "We did it, Charlie, we did it!" "Well, I'll be . . . Are you all right, Rosie?" "Never better. And you, dear?" "Bit of all right." "I'm all turned around, Charlie. Which way is the south shore?" "The one we're swimming towards, old girl."

John Huston wrote: "Katie and he were just funny together, one calling forth that quality in the other, and the combination of their two characterizations brought out the humor of dramatic situations which originally none of us thought existed. Basically, the humor underlies the story, for it's a case of the little worm of a man who turns or the prim spinster suddenly becoming the captain of the ship. But it doesn't come out of the printed page. It was the surprising combination of Hepburn and Bogart which enabled the comedy to emerge."

Bogart also recalled some fond moments working in Africa with Hepburn. "The first day on location, she acted like she was still on the MGM lot. First she demanded a private dressing room, then a full-length mirror. I thought, God, this woman. Here we are a million miles from nowhere, sleeping in bamboo huts, and she wants her studio dressing room with ankle-deep rugs and a star on the door. To keep her happy, we rigged up a sort of Chic Sale dressing shack, floated it on oil drums, and towed it upstream to location every morning and back again every night."

His opinion changed after working with her for a few days. "Although she's convinced she can do anything as well as a man, you never feel she's 'leading' you before the camera. After all my years in the movies, I'm used to dames who like their close-ups big and soft-lighted and frequent. But Katie even suggested once that only the back of her neck be shot in a scene where I'm talking."

And finally, this Bogart observation: "In the eight hundred dollar dresses she treats as rags, no one is sexier than Katie, especially before a movie camera, and you remember she has legs like Dietrich. The twenty years since you saw them on the stage in *The Warrior's Husband* haven't hurt them at all. You brand as rank slander the crack that you can throw a hat at Katie and it'll hang wherever it hits."

Many years later, Hepburn said of Bogart: "He was one of the few men I've ever known who was proud of being an actor. He thought acting was a fine profession. . . . He watched out for me, like a father, when we made *The African Queen.* A total gentleman." And recalling Bogart at the end: "I went to call on him that last night. Spencer was there, and Frank Sinatra. When we left, and Spencer shook his hand and said, 'Goodnight,' Bogey said, 'Goodbye.' Spencer was absolutely shattered, and he said, 'Bogey knows he's going to die tonight.' And the next morning he was gone."

The African Queen became one of the screen's great films and remains a favorite among Bogart fans. Jack Cardiff's outstanding photography helped establish him among the top cinematographers in the industry and opened the door a few years later to a career as a major director. The film received four Oscar nominations: Best Actor, Best Actress, Best Director, and Best Screenplay. Bogart won his only Academy Award for his performance as Charlie Allnut.

The wrap-up of Katharine Hepburn's long MGM contract came with the filming of *Pat and Mike* (1952), which reassembled the highly successful team of Tracy and Hepburn, the Kanins, and George Cukor. Returning to the studio after her African jaunt, Hepburn found Louis B. Mayer gone. Dore Schary was in command. He was paring the

PAT AND MIKE (1952). With Spencer Tracy

studio roster, cutting loose "more stars than there are in the heavens," as MGM's press department had proudly boasted for so long. Tracy continued at the studio for another three years, completing two decades in the Culver City film factory.

In *Pat and Mike,* Hepburn played a physical education teacher and vigorous lady athlete opposite Tracy's hard-boiled sports promoter - turned - manager. She had the opportunity to display her real-life expertise in swimming, golf, tennis, judo, basketball, etc. Garson Kanin had come to the conclusion, after watching in early 1952 a tennis match between Hepburn and a pro, that the actress' audience

PAT AND MIKE (1952). With
Spencer Tracy

might enjoy seeing her at play.
He suggested to his wife, Ruth
Gordon, the idea in which their
good friend could display her
athletic prowess, and *Pat and
Mike* was the result. The sports
promoter role for Tracy was a
blend of several of Kanin's New
York acquaintances.

The key line used by MGM in
its advertising campaign, more
or less taken from the film's dialogue, was Tracy's comment:
"She ain't got much meat on
her . . . but what she's got is
cherce!" Tracy, as Mike Cono-
van, offers that appraisal of
Hepburn, as Pat Pemberton, on
the golf course. The summation

is made as she is walking away
from him, and he is about to
partake of a drink from a water
fountain. Earlier, at their first
meeting, when he and one of his
pals turn up as uninvited
guests in the lady athlete's
room, he unabashedly admits to
her: "I'm here to tell you you
are one *beautiful* thing to watch
—in action!"

After she agrees to accept him
as her professional manager, the
two go to dinner at Lindy's Restaurant (in New York) where he
proceeds to run down the list of
do's and don't's (mostly don't's)
he expects her to observe as an
athlete in training, and then he
orders her meal, over her objections. "Don't forget to throw me
over your shoulder and burp me
after lunch," she tells him sar-
castically. "I will if I have to,"
he replies.

As in a great many of their
films, *Pat and Mike* is a love
story about two improbably mismatched people who defy the
odds by emerging totally com-
patible. In the film, as director
Cukor has pointed out, the two
hardly ever touch, so discreet is
their relationship. Hepburn
gives Tracy a friendly kiss on the
cheek (which he tries to wipe
away with his handkerchief and
then furtively puts the handkerchief into an inner pocket for

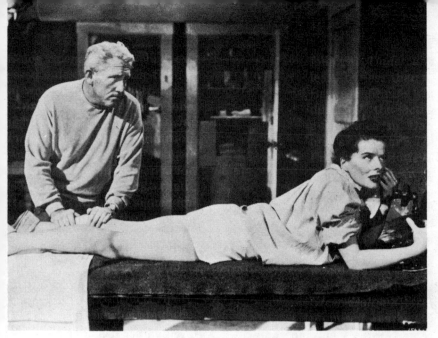

PAT AND MIKE (1952). With Spencer Tracy

safekeeping). The only truly physical contact occurs when Tracy massages Hepburn's leg to relieve a muscle strain. Since *Pat and Mike* was created in a semi-Runyonesque style, the actor had one of his rare opportunities to demonstrate his technique at broad comedy. "See her face," he tells Sammy White, referring to Hepburn. "It's a real honest face. It's the only disgusting thing about her."

Hepburn, on the other hand, had the opportunity in *Pat and Mike* to play against a number of top sports pros, such as Gussie Moran, Babe Didrikson Zaharias, Alice Marble, and Helen Dettweiler.

In addition to earning another Best Original Screenplay nomination for Ruth Gordon and Garson Kanin, the film helped the careers of Aldo Ray, whose foghorn voice suited him perfectly as the numbskull fighter Tracy is managing; Chuck Connors, the former major league first-baseman; and Charles Buchinski, who subsequently changed his surname to Bronson.

Pat and Mike, which was released during the summer of 1952, four months after *The African Queen,* brought to an end the second phase of Katharine Hepburn's screen career.

Katharine Hepburn's departure from MGM concluded the final long-term contract of her career. From 1952 onward, she would remain a true independent, choosing scripts as they interested her and dealing with producers as they contacted her. In the succeeding two decades, she starred in ten films. For them, she received six Academy Award nominations—an incredible average.

Immediately following *Pat and Mike,* there might have been another film with Tracy, Cukor, Garson Kanin, and Ruth Gordon: *The Actress,* based on Miss Gordon's autobiographical play, *Years Ago.* Had Hepburn decided not to return to the stage, she, rather than Teresa Wright, might have played young Ruth Gordon's mother.

In any event, Hepburn answered the call of Michael Benthall (he had staged her *As You Like It*), and she went to London in the spring of 1952 to star as Epifania in the first major production of George Bernard Shaw's *The Millionairess.* Shaw had written the comedy about this spoiled, pampered heiress in 1935, especially for Edith Evans, who rejected it. It was subsequently introduced at the Malverne Festival by Sybil Thorndike. In the early 1940s, a film version had been rumored

THE INDEPENDENT YEARS

for Katharine Hepburn. *The Millionairess* was finally realized on the screen in 1960, with Sophia Loren in the lead.

The play was a critical failure; Hepburn was an artistic success. One British paper commented: "Hepburn plays Shaw—and wins." W. A. Darlington, critic of the *London Daily Telegraph,* summed up: "Nobody else that I can remember has appeared in a play for which hardly any critic has a good word and by sheer personal vitality has bludgeoned her way to success." Since this was Hepburn's London debut, it seems understandable that the English critics were unaware that the word "failure" was nonexistent in the actress' lexicon. To paraphrase one of the lines from *The Philadelphia Story,* "Hepburn wouldn't stand for it."

The Millionairess was performed in London from June 27 to September 20 and then was brought to New York for a tenweek "limited engagement" at the Shubert Theater beginning October 10. John Mason Brown, writing in *Saturday Review,*

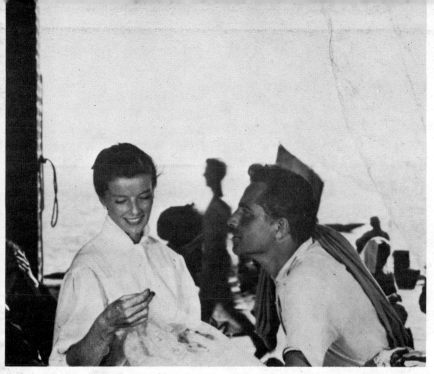

SUMMERTIME (1955). With Rossano Brazzi

said: "Miss Hepburn's contribution must be catalogued as a workout no less than a characterization. . . . Everything (she) is asked to do she does gallantly. She moves with incredible grace, and, as always, is fascinating to watch. In a part which as written is so aggressively Johnny-One-Note, she does what is perhaps unavoidable and matches the lack of variety in the writing with a lack of variety in her playing. Her stamina is amazing. Even so, though she shows no signs of wearing herself out, just watching her and listening to her

exhausted me halfway through the evening."

Eric Bentley wrote in *New Republic:* "The Millionairess is a frustrated ruler. Her frustrations are ugly, her nature is not. The cardinal error of Miss Hepburn's 'interpretation' is to make Epifinia repulsive to the core."

Following the final Hepburn performance of the Shaw play, just after Christmas, 1952, the actress faded from public view for nearly eighteen months. It was David Lean who received credit for reviving the screen Hepburn and revitalizing her in-

SUMMERTIME (1955). As Jane Hudson

terest in films and the public's interest in her. Lean brought her to Venice to star in *Summertime* (1955). This is the bittersweet love story of a lonely American spinster-teacher who, while on vacation in Europe, meets a charming Continential businessman and finds fleeting happiness in a gossamer romance. Lean and H. E. Bates had adapted the Arthur Laurents play *The Time of the Cuckoo* in which Shirley Booth had starred on Broadway at the

same time Hepburn was doing *The Millionairess.* They softened the harsh focus of the stage version and created one of the outstanding "women-oriented" screenplays of the decade, with Venice as a breathtaking backdrop. *Saturday Review* commented that "even this visually superb pageant benefits from having Katharine Hepburn in the foreground."

Hepburn's Jane Hudson, the first of the "spinster" roles for which she was to virtually corner the film market in succeeding years, is a lady who falls in love for the first time in her life but finds the future impossible after learning that the man is married and has a grown son. She makes the most of the situation—having loved, at the very least. Interwoven with the ill-starred romance between Jane Hudson and Renato Di Rossi (Rossano Brazzi), proprietor of a Venetian antique shop, is Jane's relationship with an appealing street urchin (Gaitano Audiero), who becomes her guide through the city. In bringing the introverted Jane out of her shell, both through her brief romance with Renato and her tours with young Mario, Hepburn created an actress' dream role, running the gamut of moods and actions from pathos to slapstick comedy —the latter demonstrated in a scene in which she backs into the Grand Canal while having her picture taken.

Hepburn's leading man, Rossano Brazzi, was not yet especially well-known in the United States, although he had played Professor Bhaer in the 1949 remake of *Little Women* and was

SUMMERTIME (1955). With Gaitano Audiero

one of the stars of *Three Coins in the Fountain,* made just prior to *Summertime.* It was only through Hepburn's efforts that Brazzi received co-star billing—above the title alongside (but not quite equal in size to) her name. The actor was later quoted as saying that he thought her amazingly independent "for a woman."

Much of the success and delight of *Summertime,* aside from Hepburn's brilliant performance and Lean's painstaking direction, must be credited to Jack Hildyard, whose outstanding photography made Venice on film only slightly less breathtaking than Venice in real life. *Summertime* had its premiere in that city at the end of May, 1955, and was initially unveiled in America later the following month. The Academy of Motion Picture Arts and Sciences gave Hepburn her sixth Best Actress nomination. (Anna Magnani won the award that year for *The Rose Tattoo.*) In 1965, *Summertime,* née *The Time of the Cuckoo,* returned to Broadway as a musical, reincarnated as *Do I Hear a Waltz?* with a score by Richard Rodgers and Stephen Sondheim. The stars were Elizabeth Allen and Sergio Franchi.

At the time *Summertime* was being released, Katharine Hepburn was touring Australia with Robert Helpmann (her co-star in *The Millionairess*) and the Old Vic Company, starring in three Shakespeare plays in repertory: *The Taming of the Shrew,* as Katharina; *Measure for Measure,* as Isabella; *The Merchant of Venice,* as Portia. On her return she and Helpmann stopped in England and got involved in a film ultimately called *The Iron Petticoat* (1956). In retrospect, the actress should never have touched down at Heathrow Airport in London.

Author Ben Hecht had written a story entitled *Not for Money,* with Katharine Hepburn in mind to play a Russian aviatrix who lands in West Germany after defecting and rapidly converts to capitalism after sampling its delights. The shadow of Garbo's *Ninotchka* loomed over the entire concept. Somewhere along the way, Bob Hope had chanced upon the story and expressed interest in it. Casting Hope and Hepburn opposite each other must have seemed as nearly inspired as the idea had been of teaming her with Bogart. The curious casting, as it happened, was the high-water mark of the entire project. Hope turned the script over to his own writers to "punch it up" and tai-

THE IRON PETTICOAT (1956). With Bob Hope

lor it to his style, at the expense, unfortunately, of his leading lady. Ben Hecht then insisted his own name be removed from the credits, which finally bore the legend, "Based on an Original Story by Harry Saltzman." Saltzman was to gain fame and financial rewards a few years later as co-producer of the James Bond films. Much of Hepburn's footage as Captain Vinka Kovelenko of the Russian Air Force apparently disappeared in a cut-

ting room at Pinewood Studios, for what she enacted on the screen, as seen at the film's premiere at the 1956 Berlin Film Festival, was not worth her stay in London. Nearly a year elapsed before the picture opened (and quietly stole away) in New York, five full months after its Los Angeles showing.

William K. Zinsser, reviewing *The Iron Petticoat* in the *New York Herald-Tribune*, spoke eloquently for many of his col-

THE IRON PETTICOAT (1956). With Bob Hope

THE RAINMAKER (1956). With Burt Lancaster

leagues: "When Miss Hepburn, encased in an army uniform that does nothing for her lissom figure, turns to Hope and says, 'I vas vorried,' she had good reason."

Ben Hecht subsequently printed an open letter in the film trade journals, disclaiming the picture and offering an apology to Katharine Hepburn and her fans. "Although her magnificent comic performance has been blow-torched out of the film," he wrote, "there is enough left of the Hepburn footage to identify her for her sharpshooters."

With Vinka Kovelenko mercifully sublimated and rapidly fading like a bad dream, Hepburn returned to Hollywood after a four-year hiatus to find waiting for her the character of Lizzie Curry, the shy Kansas

THE RAINMAKER (1956). With Cameron Prud'Homme, Lloyd Bridges and Earl Holliman

spinster. Like *Summertime*, her film *The Rainmaker* (1956) was based on a Broadway play; like *Summertime*, it would earn her still another Oscar nomination; like *Summertime*, it would later become a Broadway musical.

The Rainmaker, which N. Richard Nash had adapted to the screen from his 1954 play, was Hepburn's only movie for Paramount. Her leading man was Burt Lancaster in the title role. He received top billing in

the third of his "woman's" trilogy for Hal Wallis—*Come Back, Little Sheba* and *The Rose Tattoo* preceded it. Ironically, the female lead in each gave an Academy Award-nominated performance.

Lizzie Curry lives with her father and two brothers on their run-down farm in the Kansas of the twenties. They have convinced her that she is plain and that she will be an old maid. In an attempt to overcome her inferiority complex, she goes to her father (Cameron Prud'Homme) and asks: "Can a woman take lessons in being a woman?" Her crush on the town sheriff (Wendell Corey) remains unspoken because of her—and his—shyness, and it is only through her unexpected relationship with Starbuck, the fast-talking con-man who sells himself to the community as a rainmaker, that she begins to believe in her dreams and is slowly transformed into a woman ready for love.

The transformation comes in a long scene in the barn of the Curry home. Starbuck weaves his own interpretation of the legend of Mélisande and decides that Lizzie should change her name to create for herself an entirely new personality. When she scoffs at him and his dreams, he shouts angrily: "If you think it's just the same thing, then I take it back about your name! Lizzie —it's just right for you. I'll tell you another name that would suit you—Noah! Because you and your brother—you've got no dream." And then she turns her tear-stained face to him and pours out her heart: "You think all dreams have to be your kind! Golden Fleece and Thunder on the Mountain! But there are other dreams, Starbuck—little quiet ones that come to a woman when she's shining the silverware and putting moth flakes in the closet. Like a man's voice saying: 'Lizzie, is my blue suit pressed?' And the same man saying: 'Scratch me between my shoulder blades.' And kids laughing and teasing and setting up a racket. And how it feels to say the word 'husband!' . . . There are all kinds of dreams, Mr. Starbuck. Mine are small ones—like my name. Lizzie. But they're *real* like my name— *real!* So you can have yours— and I'll have mine!" "Melisande," she decides, "is a name for one night, but Lizzie will do me for my whole life long."

The Rainmaker was released in December, 1956, two weeks before America had its initial (west coast) glimpse of *The Iron Petticoat.* Reviewing her performance as Lizzie Curry, *Time* commented: "Actress Hepburn does not always suggest the stages in Lizzie's life, as she passes from emotional chrysalis to vivid imaginal maturity, but she holds the eye in scene after scene like a brilliant moth as she batters wildly about one or another light o' love."

The Rainmaker brought an Oscar nomination to Alex North for his score as well as to Hepburn as Best Actress. The film

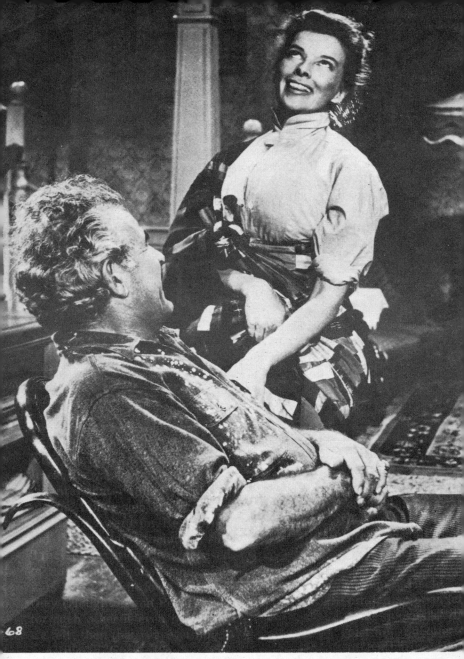

THE RAINMAKER (1956). With Cameron Prud'Homme

106

DESK SET (1957). With Spencer Tracy

was directed by Joseph Anthony, who had also staged the Broadway version with Geraldine Page and Darren McGavin. The 1963 musical adaptation was called *110 in the Shade*. Its score was by Harvey Schmidt and Tom Jones; its stars were Inga Swenson and Robert Horton.

Hepburn once again costarred with Spencer Tracy, enacting in *Desk Set* another role originated on Broadway (in 1955) by Shirley Booth. She did her only work on the 20th Century-Fox soundstages in this adaptation by Phoebe and Henry Ephron of William Marchant's lightweight

DESK SET (1957). With Joan Blondell and Spencer Tracy

comedy. She plays a television researcher who fears that she and many of her colleagues are about to be replaced by a computer, and it was generally agreed that she got more out of the part than the concept really deserved. Tracy is the engineer who designed this "evil" electronic brain and is the misunderstood villain of the piece.

Producer and coauthor Henry Ephron have recalled one of the sight gags involving the indomitable Miss Hepburn and a giant philodendron. "She came to the set, looked at a giant-sized plant we had there, and said: 'That's not a philodendron.' The set director (Walter M. Scott) said it was; she said it wasn't. We called in the studio gardener who said it was; she said it wasn't. Finally she left, and the same afternoon, she staggered back with a twenty-year-old rented philodendron that was too big for the Fox elevator and had to be lugged upstairs. 'That's a philodendron!' she said. It was, and we used it."

Leon Shamroy photographed *Desk Set* so lovingly that Hepburn looked not a day older than she had in *Pat and Mike* five years earlier, and director Walter Lang creatively captured to the letter Hepburn's opinion —and that of most critics and fans: "On screen, I think Spencer and I are the perfect American couple." Her Bunny Watson, the walking catalogue of the network's reference library, is totally out of tune with his Richard Sumner, whose computer has the answer to everything. As in the previous Tracy-Hepburn teamings, the situation —competition between the two to determine the better man—is the same; only the details are rearranged. In support of the stars are Gig Young, recreating his nearly patented role of "the other man who loses the girl but never his disarming grin"; Joan Blondell, in another of her familiar wise-cracking, heart-of-gold, life-of-the-office performances; and Dina Merrill, Sue Randall, Neva Patterson, and the screen's representative sweet little old lady, Ida Moore.

Apart from being a diverting and expensive piece of fluff offering the circumstances for Tracy and Hepburn to work together, *Desk Set* proved one vital fact which became quite clear. In critic Bosley Crowther's words, "Miss Hepburn obviously is a woman who is superior to a thinking machine."

After completing *Desk Set*, Hepburn returned home to Connecticut where she spent the summer performing Shakespeare

DESK SET (1957). With Spencer Tracy

at Stratford. For three weeks in July, she played Portia in *The Merchant of Venice;* for three weeks in August, she was Beatrice in *Much Ado About Nothing.* John Chapman, drama critic for the *New York Daily News,* said of her Portia: "(She) is no mere lovely picture; she is a girl of intelligence, humor, and iron determination—which is almost type-casting."

Now that she had indulged herself in both Shakespeare and Shaw, Hepburn decided to tackle Tennessee Williams and Eugene O'Neill. For her efforts, she received her eighth and ninth Oscar nominations. In 1959, she returned to England to star with Elizabeth Taylor and Montgomery Clift in the screen version of the short play by Williams, *Suddenly, Last Summer* (1959). The call to Hepburn came from Joseph L. Mankiewicz, who had produced both *The Philadelphia Story* and *Woman of the Year* and had since become an important director, reversing the usual process.

Suddenly, Last Summer formed the basis for a mutual admiration society between Hepburn and Williams. To prepare for the film, according to Garson Kanin, the actress spent a great amount of time making a complete study of the works of the noted author. Williams, on the other hand, was in the process of turning his short story *Night of the Iguana* into a play specifically for Hepburn, hoping she would perform in it during the forthcoming Broadway season. Unfortunately, she was committed to a return engagement at the American Shakespeare Festival during 1960.

Gore Vidal collaborated with Williams on the screen version of the play, originally produced off-Broadway in early 1958 along with another of the author's short works, *Something Unspoken*. Both were presented under the collective title, *Garden District*. Anne Meacham, Hortense Alden, and Robert Lansing played on stage the roles Taylor, Hepburn, and Clift interpreted on screen.

Suddenly, Last Summer is a series of monologues which dovetail into a study in depravity. Hepburn's Mrs. Venable is a vicious woman, in love with her deceased homosexual son and trying to have a frontal lobotomy performed on her lovely niece (Taylor) to protect that secret, and the fact that she, and later the unsuspecting niece, pimped for him. Clift is the young brain surgeon who demands to learn the truth before accepting Mrs. Venable's one million-dollar offer to perform the operation. Throughout the film, Hepburn is clad in white mourning. She makes a grand entrance, descending in the private elevator of her exotic home which is replete with tropical gardens and insectivorous plants to which she gleefully feeds daily rations of flies. Her character is succinctly established in her very first line to the doctor: "Are you interested in the Byzantine?"

Suddenly, Last Summer was a shocker and it pioneered the liberal movement which was to overtake the film industry during the next decade. The Hepburn performance brought the actress more diverse critical appraisals than almost any screen interpretation she had given since her RKO days. *Newsweek* wrote: "As the domineering and eccentric Mrs. Venable, (she)

SUDDENLY, LAST SUMMER (1959). With Montgomery Clift

managed to overlay her cultured voice effectively with touches of the stuttering 'method' style of acting; she is a sheer wonder, and if she were any better, she would be preposterous." *The London Observer's* C. A. Lejune thought she "acts brilliantly but privately, as though she'd never realised there were other persons in the picture." And Arthur Knight wrote in *Saturday Review:* "Katharine Hepburn uses every ounce of the Hepburn charm (and every one of the Hepburn mannerisms) to make her portrait of an egocentric matron and too-doting mother ring true."

Hepburn was said to have been quite disturbed during the filming because of the way an obviously ill Montgomery Clift was being treated, and she blamed both director Mankiewicz and producer Sam Spiegel, complaining strongly to both at the close of production.

In addition to the Oscar nomination for Hepburn, there was one for Elizabeth Taylor, and Oliver Messel and William Kellner were nominated for their art direction and Scott Simon for his evocative sets. The striking color photography by Jack Hildyard, who also had shot *Summertime,* was overlooked by the Academy. The film, in-cidentally, was unique in Hepburn's career in that she took second billing to another actress.

Suddenly, Last Summer was followed by a second summer of Shakespeare in Stratford, Connecticut. Next she portrayed Mary Tyrone in the film version of Eugene O'Neill's *Long Day's Journey Into Night* (1962). O'Neill had written this autobiographical work in 1941, but had stipulated that it not be produced until after his death. It was given its first Broadway production in November, 1956, five years after O'Neill died. The stars were Fredric March, Florence Eldridge, Jason Robards Jr., and Bradford Dillman. The film adaptation was under the direction of Sidney Lumet. In addition to Katharine Hepburn playing the drug-addicted mother, the cast included Ralph Richardson, as the father who had once been an important Shakespearean actor; Jason Robards Jr., recreating his stage role as the drunken older brother Jamie; and Dean Stockwell as young Edmund Tyrone, actually the twenty - three - year - old O'Neill.

Producer Ely Landau related to Hollywood columnist Sheilah Graham how he got Katharine Hepburn to accept her role. "I called Miss Hepburn and said,

SUDDENLY, LAST SUMMER (1959). As Violet Venable

SUDDENLY, LAST SUMMER (1959). With Montgomery Clift and Elizabeth Taylor

'My name is Ely Landau and I'm going into motion picture production, and I'd like you to do a picture for me.' 'Who are you?' she asked. I told her my name again and said that among other things I had produced *Play of the Week* on television. 'Oh, what are you considering?' she asked. I told her. She replied, 'I've been interested in the play for years. Who will do the screenplay?' 'Eugene O'Neill,' I told her. There was a long pause, then she said, 'That's marvel-ous. When do you expect to do it?' 'Next month,' I told her. 'Mr. Landau, I think you're nuts; we don't do things that way,' she commented."

Beginning in the autumn of 1961, director Lumet shot the film in sequence over a period of only 37 days. The budget was $400,000, including $25,000 (more or less) in salaries plus a share of any profits for each of the four principals. Hepburn later said: "I've never been much interested in money. I don't give a damn

LONG DAY'S JOURNEY INTO NIGHT (1962). With Ralph Richardson

LONG DAY'S JOURNEY INTO NIGHT (1962). With Dean Stockwell, Ralph Richardson and Jason Robards Jr.

about clothes and I don't care about possessions. I've gotten tremendous fees when the material was boring, and the only time I've ever really kicked myself is when I've done something I didn't want to do just because of the money involved." For her two previous acting assignments, she had received $300 a week playing Shakespeare and approximately $175,000 (to Taylor's $250,000) for her interpretation of Williams' Violet Venable.

Eugene O'Neill set the action in *Long Day's Journey Into Night* in New London, Connecticut (it was filmed in the Bronx and in Manhattan's Production Center Studios on West 26th

Street), in 1912, on the day that Mary Tyrone resumes taking drugs, Edmund learns that he has tuberculosis, and James and James, Jr. drink themselves into stupefaction. With some slight condensation of the original play and an acceleration of pacing, the four hour and twenty minute marathon drama, with three intermissions, was reduced to two hours and fifty-seven minutes. Among the cuts: the opening five or six minutes, a few poetic quotations, and snippets from the longer speeches.

Lumet gave the action fluidity by inserting effective bits of business, such as having Mary Tyrone rolling about on the floor in a morphine stupor, James Tyrone combing his stage wig, father and son puttering about in the tool shed.

Lumet drew powerful performances from all four and in an interview shortly after the film's release, Hepburn admitted: "It's far damn well the best thing I ever did. I never had such an interesting time in my life. We all liked each other enormously— but not too much. You can have a wonderful time and a flop *that* way. I don't think I got in the way of it."

Katharine Hepburn crowned her performance as Mary Tyrone with the moving and tragic final night scene, looking for all the world like an aging Ophelia, descending the staircase wearing her faded wedding gown. (Note the parallel to the final scene in *Suddenly, Last Summer* when she ascends in her elevator wearing her white mourning outfit.) She tries desperately to remain lucid in her narcotic stupor and seeks from somewhere and nowhere answers that elude her. "What is it I'm looking for? I know, it's something I lost. . . . Something I need terribly." And at the end, there is recollection, of her painful last day at the convent when the Mother Superior sent her home to experience life. "That was in the winter of the senior year. Then in the spring something happened to me. Yes, I remember, I fell in love with James Tyrone and was so happy for a time."

The film was first shown at the 1962 Cannes Film Festival (its American premiere was the following October) and the four principals were voted an ensemble "Best Acting" award, unique for the prestigious festival. Hepburn was subsequently nominated for her ninth Oscar.

Long Day's Journey Into Night was not for the taste of every filmgoer. As a low budget "art" film, boasting big names, the production had an admitted

LONG DAY'S JOURNEY INTO NIGHT (1962). As Mary Tyrone

limited appeal. It opened at a small house on the exclusive East Side of Manhattan and enjoyed a long engagement. Low budget or not, it was an important motion picture, and the critics gave it especially detailed analyses. Of Hepburn's interpretation of the mother, Pauline Kael wrote: "The most beautiful comedienne of the thirties and forties has become our greatest tragedienne." The critic continued: "Experiencing the magic in the art of acting, one can understand why the appellation 'the divine' has sometimes been awarded to certain actresses." Arthur Knight said in *Saturday Review:* "Katharine Hepburn caps her distinguished career in the role of the pitiful, dope-addicted mother, groping back to the past for dimly remembered moments of happiness."

Following *Long Day's Journey Into Night,* Hepburn was not seen professionally for nearly five years, emerging only briefly for David O. Selznick's funeral in June, 1965, and reading Rudyard Kipling's *If* to the gathering. Her inactivity, it later became evident, was enforced in order to devote herself to the ailing Spencer Tracy. Around this time, Hepburn publicly summed up her relationship with Tracy in one line: "I have had twenty years of perfect companionship with a man among men."

It was because of Tracy that she accepted the invitation of producer-director Stanley Kramer, who had directed him in four of the actor's last five films, to resume her career with Spencer in *Guess Who's Coming to Dinner,* in 1967. A second reason for consenting was the screen debut of her niece, Katharine Houghton, who was not to make another film for more than six years. For the first time in her career, Katharine Hepburn received *third* billing after both Tracy and Sidney Poitier. She said: "Spencer and I agreed to do the picture as soon as Stanley Kramer brought it to us. The idea is good and true. I suppose it will disturb some people and raise a fuss, but fifty or a hundred years from now, I don't think this picture will be shocking at all, because we'll be practicing intermarriage."

Shooting on the film began in February with deep concern and crossed-fingers all around. Tracy had been ill, but he was determined to get through *Guess Who's Coming To Dinner,* his seventy-fourth film. He admitted it would be his last. Many stories about the production have been written—how Katharine Hepburn nearly drove

GUESS WHO'S COMING TO DINNER (1967). With Sidney Poitier and Spencer Tracy

GUESS WHO'S COMING TO DINNER (1967). With Sidney Poitier, Katharine Houghton and Spencer Tracy

Stanley Kramer to distraction with her "fussiness" on the set, knowing not only her own lines but everybody else's, as well as all the stage directions, the camera angles, and the written and unwritten bits of business. In her own mind, however, she was there not only to give a performance but also to give moral and physical support to Tracy and to her sister Marion's daughter in her first film role.

In addition to playing a loving wife and mother for the first time on the screen, Hepburn was on hand in more than one scene to literally hold up the ailing Tracy while he delivered his lines. It was by no means accidental that William Rose's dialogue (for which he won the Academy Award for Best Original Screenplay) included this Tracy observation when accused of no longer remembering what it is like to be in love: "If what they (Houghton and Poitier) feel for each other is even half what *we* felt, then that is everything."

Although *Guess Who's Coming To Dinner* is strictly Tracy's

film, down to the farewell speech (actually shot first) directed at the audience, which earned him his ninth Oscar nomination—the most among actors, it was Hepburn who won the Academy Award for, frankly, a pedestrian role. She has been quoted as saying: "I'm sure mine is for the two of us."

Had Tracy lived, it is agreed that he probably would have been awarded the Oscar, but it never has been bestowed posthumously. A fact of business reality stemming from an unwritten proposition that a dead man can be of no future assistance at the boxoffice.

In *Guess Who's Coming To Dinner,* Hepburn and Tracy play Christina and Matt Drayton, the liberal, socially prominent parents (she operates an avant-garde art gallery and he is a newspaper publisher) of an attractive young girl who returns from a Hawaiian vacation with a guest in tow—a black doctor. Christina and Matt find their principles put to the test when asked to give their blessings to an interracial marriage.

Rather than face the issues head-on, screenwriter William Rose gave the subject a superficial treatment and couched the proceedings in a witty stream of dialogue, while director Kramer put his actors through the paces with polish and style. Among the many carping remarks made about the film was that Sidney Poitier's doctor had the credentials for sainthood let alone the hand in marriage of such an important person as the daughter of Katharine Hepburn and Spencer Tracy. Poitier was made to be a Rhodes scholar, a United Nations consultant, a Nobel Prize candidate, a distinguished surgeon—and, of course, brilliant, charming, and good looking. However, because it was the first major film to tackle—however diffidently—such an important and controversial contemporary subject, it remains a milestone in motion picture history. In the film, Hepburn herself sums up the liberal attitude in a confrontation with her close friend and business partner (Virginia Christine) whom she discovers to be a bigot, and finally tells her to pack her belongings at the gallery and get out. It was a true audience-rouser and revealed that the independent Hepburn had not lost her fire. She and Tracy also brought innumerable personal touches to the story—a look here, an "Oh!" there, the simple purchase of an ice cream cone with a long-remembered flavor.

In addition to Oscar nomina-

GUESS WHO'S COMING TO DINNER (1967). With Spencer Tracy

tions for Tracy, Hepburn, and William Rose, the film received seven others: Best Picture, Best Director, Best Supporting Actor (Cecil Kellaway as the family priest and friend), Best Supporting Actress (Beah Richards as Poitier's concerned mother), Best Editing, Best Art Direction, and Best Musical Score. Oddly, Poitier, who had starred in two other important 1967 films—*In the Heat of the Night* and *To Sir, With Love*—was overlooked for all three roles, and much disappointment was voiced, especially among the black community.

The last day of filming on *Guess Who's Coming To Dinner*

was May 26. At the traditional on-set party, which Tracy was unable to attend, Hepburn made a rare speech to the crew: "I don't think you people realize how dependent we are on you for the encouragement you give us. These are the things that make up our lives. You are the people who make an actor able to act, and I don't know how many of you realize that. But I know that your help made a hell of a lot of difference to Spence."

Following Spencer Tracy's death two weeks later, there was speculation that Hepburn would once again retire from the screen. Rather, she plunged back to work with seemingly renewed fervor, travelling to Ireland and to France to film *The Lion in Winter* (1968), based on James Goldman's 1966 play starring Robert Preston and Rosemary Harris. Peter O'Toole personally flew to Los Angeles to ask Hepburn to accept the role of Eleanor of Aquitaine opposite his King Henry II.

In early 1968, the cast, under director Anthony Harvey, began two weeks of rehearsals on the stage of London's Haymarket Theatre prior to the actual start of production. The screenplay, also by James Goldman, was compared by *The London Observer* to "a medieval variant on *The Little Foxes,*" dealing in this case with the twelfth-century chess game among Henry II, his wife Eleanor, and their sons Richard, Geoffrey, and John, along with Henry's mistress and her brother, over the question of succession. To discuss the family problem, Henry has brought to his castle at Chinon the wife whom he had imprisoned ten years earlier for meddling in affairs of state. Hepburn made another of her splendid grand entrances, majestically seated on a barge drifting slowly up river into the dim sunshine, to begin this Yuletide family reunion. Throughout their meeting, the independent Eleanor continues venting her venom, while Henry flaunts his love for his mistress (Jane Merrow). Simultaneously the haughty, aging queen desperately tries to arrange a hasty marriage between their son Richard (Anthony Hopkins) and Henry's mistress.

Hepburn managed to get off some of the movie's best lines: "Hush, dear, mother's fighting," and "Well, what family doesn't have its ups and downs," while such matters as incest, sodomy, patricide, and treason run rampant. Hepburn said of her character: "Eleanor must have been tough as nails to have lived to be

THE LION IN WINTER (1968). With Peter O'Toole

eighty-two years old and full of beans. Both she and Henry were probably bigtime operators who played for whole countries. I like bigtime operators."

Writing in *New York* magazine, Judith Crist enthused: "Miss Hepburn certainly crowns her career as Eleanor, triumphant in her creation of a complete and womanly queen, a vulture mother who sees her sons too clearly, an aging beauty who can look her image in the eye, a sophisticate whose shrewdness is matched only by her humor." Like virtually all of Hepburn's directors, Anthony Harvey has been asked his opinion of his leading lady. His comment: "Working with her is like going to Paris at the age of seventeen and finding everything is the way you thought it would be."

Peter O'Toole, recreating the role of Henry II (much aged) which he had done in *Becket,* was nominated for an Academy Award, as he was also for *Becket.* Katharine Hepburn re-

THE LION IN WINTER (1968). With Peter O'Toole

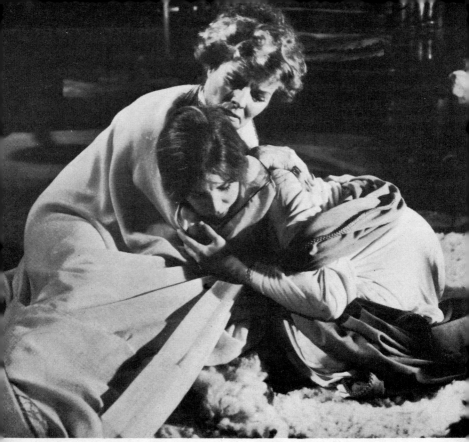

THE LION IN WINTER (1968). With Jane Merrow

ceived an unprecedented eleventh nomination—and won the Award for the third time, sharing it with Barbra Streisand.

During the filming of *The Lion in Winter,* Katharine Hepburn agreed to violate her long-standing decision not to appear on television, for the Academy Award presentations to be made in the spring of 1968. She, of course, had been invited as a nominee. She spoke on film of the first ten years of the Oscar in one of four segments covering the Awards' four decades. She was dressed as Eleanor of Aquitaine.

John Huston then convinced Hepburn to star for him in the film version of Jean Giraudoux's fragile 1948 fantasy, *The Madwoman of Chaillot* (1969). An

THE LION IN WINTER (1968). With Peter O'Toole

THE MADWOMAN OF CHAILLOT (1969). With Margaret Leighton and Giulietta Masina

impressive cast of international names was announced, a number of whom subsequently left, along with director Huston, who at least shot the first seventeen days. Hepburn remained, with, among others, Charles Boyer—her leading man three decades earlier in *Break of Hearts*. Ely Landau, who had induced Hepburn to accept the role of Mary Tyrone in *Long Day's Journey Into Night*, put up the money for the production which was filmed in Nice on a $250,000 set representing the Chaillot quarter of Paris. The film was visually stunning but it

was top-heavy with talent and collapsed under its own weight and its multi-million dollar budget.

The Madwoman of Chaillot had been a wispy enough concept to begin with—a dotty old countess and her eccentric friends decide to save the world from avarice and corruption. Hepburn's interpretation was warm, sentimental, and wise. Perhaps it was the screenplay by Edward Anhalt or Bryan Forbes' direction, but it simply did not work on film. Hepburn in her boas and feathers (which led the *New York Times* critic Vincent

Canby to comment: "Miss Hepburn's Marie Antoinette hats use more feathers than Josephine Baker would have worn as entire gowns.") was just not mad enough—but she could still manage a great weeping act!

In 1967, shortly after Tracy's death, Hepburn was approached by Alan Jay Lerner to star in a musical which he and Andre Previn were writing on the life of famed fashion designer, Gabrielle 'Coco' Chanel. Sometime later, when Garson Kanin asked the reason for Hepburn's quick acceptance, she commented: "Because it's the first time in my life anyone wanted me for my voice." Between the filming of *The Lion in Winter* and *The Madwoman of Chaillot,* the actress worked with Roger Eden, who had been accompaniest to Ethel Merman, Judy Garland and other musical stars and was associate producer of the film version of *Hello, Dolly!* At Irene Mayer Selznick's apartment at the Hotel Pierre in New York, an intimate party had as its entertainment, one night in mid-1968, a truly unique concert. Hepburn gave her first recital of songs by Cole Porter, and Lerner and Loewe. *Coco* was undergoing its birth pangs. Lerner noted: "She's remarkably musical and, unlike most actors who forget to act when they sing, she was always acting."

Hepburn's return to the stage after seventeen years—and in a musical—became one of the most eagerly awaited events of the 1969-70 theatre season. It was agreed at the outset that Hepburn might not have been the ideal choice to play Gabrielle Chanel during the fashion trendsetter's later years—actually, Claudette Colbert would have been closer, according to most knowledgable critics' impressions of the designer. *Coco,* as a show, was far less than the greatest event in the annals of Broadway—the book was tedious and the score mediocre. But Katharine Hepburn's presence alone made it the most expensive musical ever staged and the largest grossing show of all time. It averaged $140,000 a week, of which the star received 10-15 percent or about $350,000 for the entire run. During the nine months she starred on Broadway in *Coco,* Hepburn never missed a performance—and there was never an empty seat at the Mark Hellinger Theatre.

Hepburn simply overwhelmed Broadway when *Coco* opened the week before Christmas, 1969. Clive Barnes wrote in the *New York Times:* "Dear Miss Hepburn—perhaps they should have

THE MADWOMAN OF CHAILLOT (1969). With John Gavin, Oscar Homolka, Paul Henreid, Charles Boyer, Yul Brynner and Donald Pleasance

made a musical of your life rather than the dress designer's. They say some beauty is ageless —yours is timeless." And *Variety's* Hobe Morrison said: "That this rampaging feminist is sensationally successful doesn't make her particularly interesting. What saves her as a stage character is Miss Hepburn, giving the performance of her life. It is an electrifying, captivating performance; a virtuoso achievement."

Hepburn was nominated for a Tony Award, and made a taped appearance on the Awards program, performing the elaborate "Always Mademoiselle" number with a stageful of mirrors. She lost the Tony Award to Lauren Bacall for *Applause*. That *Coco* was dependent on Katharine Hepburn for its survival was proved when she left the Broadway production on August 1, 1970. Replacing her in the title role was Danielle Darrieux—infinitely more plausible as Mme. Chanel. She was unable, however, to attract an audience, and the show limped along for two more months before closing. Following a brief rest and another film to which she already had committed herself, Hepburn returned to *Coco*, taking the show on a six-month national tour, beginning in Cleveland on January 11, 1971, and ending at the Chandler Pavilion in Los Angeles on June 26. She drew capacity audiences wherever she played, as she had done on Broadway.

Between the two productions of *Coco*, Hepburn had chosen to play Hecuba, the aged queen of Troy, in Michael Cacoyannis' version of Euripides' *The Trojan Women* (1971). Replete with its location atmosphere (Atienza, Spain, turned into the Troy of the fourth century B.C.), the screen version is actually filmed theatre, with long, static stretches of dialogue confrontations and a multitude of black-cloaked women. It was a large-scale, somewhat expanded version of the production staged by Cacoyannis in 1963 at Circle-in-the-Square off-Broadway.

The movie relies on the acting abilities of its players, and a greater range of styles, accents, and attitudes would be difficult to imagine. In addition to Hepburn, Vanessa Redgrave was signed to play Andromache, Genevieve Bujold was cast as Cassandra (Hecuba's daughter), and Irene Papas was given the role of Helen, whose face, according to legend, launched a thousand ships. With this casting, promise was held forth of a daz-

As Coco Chanel in COCO (1969/1970)

zling display of histrionics among the quartet of dynamic ladies. If Hepburn as a Greek queen was any more bizarre than Hepburn as a Russian pilot or a Chinese peasant or even as a boy, it is to her credit that she even attempted the illusion.

The Euripides tragedy, which opens with the end of the Trojan War, deals basically with three major episodes, each centering on the fate of one of the captives. All three are linked by the central character of Hecuba (Hepburn), who must withstand a wide range of catastrophes before her subjugation into slavery.

On the whole, the film was not well-received by the critics. Writing in the *New York Times,* Vincent Canby called it "high-class mediocre" and said it was "compounded by a series of casting coups that look like the remains of thirty years of Miss Universe contests." He appraised the Hepburn performance this way: "(She) plays old, gray-headed Hecuba not so much like the defeated Queen of Troy she is supposed to be but more like an apple grower's widow who weeps a lot . . . (she) speaks most of her lines with small, elegant accents that have very little to do with epic grief, and only in her final confrontation with Helen, the one who has brought ruin down upon them all, does her Hecuba suggest real depth and passion."

After completing her national tour with *Coco* in 1971, Hepburn had been scheduled to work in films once again with George Cukor in the screen version of Graham Greene's *Travels with My Aunt.* She left the project in February, 1972, over what were simply termed "artistic differences." She was replaced by Maggie Smith. Various projects still remained on the Hepburn calendar in the early seventies. Her plans to debut as a movie director with her long-time friend, Irene Mayer Selznick, as producer—announced in a story in the *New York Times* as far back as October, 1968—have yet to materialize. The initial project was to have been *Martha,* based on two related novels by British author Margery Sharp. At the time, Hepburn said: "This isn't a fantasy. I, too, loved the books in which the heroine is a vigorous, opinionated girl, exactly like me. But it's thirty years too late for me to play the role. The fact is I've always been interested in directing—Louis B. Mayer quite seriously asked me to direct films twenty years ago, as did John Ford, the director—but I've never had a real opportunity

THE TROJAN WOMEN (1971). With Vanessa Redgrave

to do so before this. I think I can do a damn good job of it."

A proposed London company of *Coco,* taking Hepburn back to the West End for the first time in two decades, also has been mentioned, as has been a film version of the Lerner-Previn musical. And in early 1972, shortly after Hepburn departed *Travels with My Aunt,* a subsequent film project dealing with the noted author, Daisy Bates, had been placed under the actress' consideration, for production in Australia. Also: Tony Richardson's film version of Edward Albee's *A Delicate Balance.*

In February, 1970, Katharine Hepburn was named by the editors of *McCall's* as its Woman of the Year. They wrote: "We honor Katharine Hepburn as a woman, not actress, though surely she is much of both. Miss Hepburn has the traditional feminine values in untraditional ways. She is a raving individual. We should have more like her."

Of herself, she has said: "I've never considered myself an actress, which is odd, because I've always been one. Maybe because I've always thrown myself into so many things the word 'actress' doesn't mean much to me." On acting, itself, this has been the Hepburn philosophy: "I always try to memorize the whole script before the picture begins. It isn't a question of discipline, but a necessity. Otherwise I don't know what I'm doing." She continued: "I can't understand actors who learn their lines *approximately.* I'm a demon about that. So was Spencer. I learn them *exactly,*

THE TROJAN WOMEN (1971). As Hecuba

THE TROJAN WOMEN (1971). With Genevieve Bujold

word for word—no 'wells' or 'buts' thrown in. If it's a good script, it means a writer has sweated over every part of it and a single word change can throw everything. If it's a bad script, you shouldn't be doing it."

Hepburn remains, as one writer put it, "one of our national treasures, like all the indestructible old girls of the early talkies." It is *the* indestructible old girl herself who has the last line: "If you survive, you become a legend. I'm a legend because I've survived over a long period of time. I'm revered rather like an old building."

As herself in 1970.

BIBLIOGRAPHY

Atkinson, Brooks. *Broadway*. The Macmillan Company, New York, 1970

Capra, Frank. *The Name Above the Title*. The Macmillan Company, New York, 1971

Deschner, Donald. *The Films of Spencer Tracy*. Citadel Press, New York, 1968.

Dickens, Homer. *The Films of Katharine Hepburn*. Citadel Press, New York, 1971

Kanin, Garson. *Tracy and Hepburn*. The Viking Press, New York, 1970

Lambert, Gavin. *On Cukor*, G. P. Putnam's Sons, New York, 1972

Nolan, William F. *John Huston, King Rebel*. Sherbourne Press, Los Angeles, 1965

Shipman, Donald. *The Great Movie Stars: The Golden Years*, Crown Publishers, New York, 1970

Swindell, Larry. *Spencer Tracy*. World Publishing Company, New York, 1969

Articles:

Collier's: "Kate the Great" by Kyle Crichton, December 4, 1943

Film Comment: "The Films of Ring Lardner Jr." by Kenneth Geist, Winter 1970-71

Films and Filming: "Katharine Hepburn" by Peter Cowie, June, 1963

Films in Review: "Katharine Hepburn" by Romano V. Tozzi, December, 1957

Films in Review: "Katharine Hepburn Since '57" by Ronald L. Bowers, August-September, 1970

Life: "The Comeback of Kate: Ageless Queen Full of Beans" by John Frook, January 5, 1968

Life: "The Hepburns" by Oliver O. Jensen, January 22, 1940

Look: "The Unsinkable Katharine Hepburn" by Peter S. Feibleman, August 6, 1968

McCall's: "Katharine Hepburn" by Roy Newquist, July, 1967

Movie: Elia Kazan Interview by Stuart Byron & Martin L. Rubin, Winter 1971-72

Newsweek: "Kate and Coco" by Hubert Saal, November 10, 1969

New York Post: "Katharine Hepburn Talks About the Right of Privacy" by Katharine Houghton Hepburn, August 15, 1965

The New York Times: "Come I Want You to Meet My Niece" by Cecilia Ager, June 18, 1967

The New York Times: "Katie, Katie, What A Lady" by Larry Swindell, April 27, 1969

The Saturday Evening Post: "The Hepburn Story" by Lupton A. Wilkinson & J. Bryan III, November 29, 1941-January 6, 1942

Time: "The Hepburn Story," September 1, 1952

THE FILMS OF
KATHARINE HEPBURN

The director's name follows the release date. A (c) following the release date indicates that the film was in color. Sp indicates Screenplay and b/o indicates based/on.

1. A BILL OF DIVORCEMENT. RKO, 1932. *George Cukor.* Sp: Howard Estabrook & Harry Wagstaff Gribble, b/o play by Clemence Dane. Cast: John Barrymore, Billie Burke, David Manners, Henry Stephenson. KH is daughter of an insane man who forsakes her own happiness to take care of him. Remade in 1940.

2. CHRISTOPHER STRONG. RKO, 1933. *Dorothy Arzner.* Sp: Zoë Akins, b/o novel by Gilbert Frankau. Cast: Colin Clive, Billie Burke, Helen Chandler, Ralph Forbes. Titled aviatrix (KH) has affair with married politician.

3. MORNING GLORY. RKO, 1933. *Lowell Sherman.* Sp: Howard J. Green, b/o unproduced play by Zoë Akins. Cast: Douglas Fairbanks Jr., Adolphe Menjou, C. Aubrey Smith, Mary Duncan. KH in Oscar-winning performance as aspiring actress. Remade as *Stage Struck* in 1958.

4. LITTLE WOMEN. RKO, 1933. *George Cukor.* Sp: Sarah Y. Mason & Victor Heerman, b/o novel by Louisa May Alcott. Cast: Joan Bennett, Paul Lukas, Edna May Oliver, Jean Parker, Frances Dee, Spring Byington, Henry Stephenson. In this screen classic KH is Jo March. Remade in 1949.

5. SPITFIRE. RKO, 1934. *John Cromwell*. Sp: Jane Murfin & Lula Vollmer, b/o play *Trigger* by Lula Vollmer. Cast: Robert Young, Ralph Bellamy, Martha Sleeper, Sara Haden. KH is tomboy faith healer of the Ozarks.

6. THE LITTLE MINISTER. RKO, 1934. *Richard Wallace*. Sp: Jane Murfin, Sarah Y. Mason & Victor Heerman, b/o novel & play by Sir James M. Barrie. Cast: John Beal, Alan Hale, Donald Crisp, Dorothy Stickney, Reginald Denny. In guise of gypsy wench, Lady Babbie (KH) woos and wins the local minister.

7. BREAK OF HEARTS. RKO, 1935. *Richard Moeller*. Sp: Sarah Y. Mason, Victor Heerman & Anthony Veiller, b/o story by Lester Cohen. Cast: Charles Boyer, John Beal, Jean Hersholt, Sam Hardy, Inez Courtney. KH is young pianist who marries a famed conductor.

8. ALICE ADAMS. RKO, 1935. *George Stevens*. Sp: Dorothy Yost & Mortimer Offner, b/o novel by Booth Tarkington. Cast: Fred MacMurray, Fred Stone, Evelyn Venable, Frank Albertson, Ann Shoemaker, Charley Grapewin, Hattie McDaniel. KH is lovelorn girl ambitious for social recognition. Her second Academy Award nomination.

9. SYLVIA SCARLETT. RKO, 1936. *George Cukor*. Sp: Gladys Unger, John Collier & Mortimer Offner, b/o novel by Compton MacKenzie. Cast: Cary Grant, Brian Aherne, Edmund Gwenn, Natalie Paley, Dennie Moore. KH, masquerading as a boy, joins a gang of Cockney swindlers.

10. MARY OF SCOTLAND. RKO, 1936. *John Ford*. Sp: Dudley Nichols, b/o play by Maxwell Anderson. Cast: Fredric March, Florence Eldridge, Douglas Watson, John Carradine, Alan Mowbray, Frieda Inescort, Donald Crisp. KH in title role.

11. A WOMAN REBELS. RKO, 1936. *Mark Sandrich*. Sp: Anthony Veiller & Ernest Vajda, b/o novel *Portrait of a Rebel* by Netta Syrett. Cast: Herbert Marshall, Elizabeth Allan, Donald Crisp, Doris Dudley, David Manners, Van Heflin, Lucile Watson. KH is Victorian leader of woman's struggle for emancipation.

12. QUALITY STREET. RKO, 1937. *George Stevens*. Sp: Mortimer Offner & Allan Scott, b/o play by Sir James M. Barrie. Cast: Franchot Tone, Fay Bainter, Eric Blore, Cora Witherspoon, Estelle Winwood, Bonita Granville, Joan Fontaine. Girl (KH) masquerades as her non-existent niece to win her man.

13. STAGE DOOR. RKO, 1937. *Gregory La Cava*. Sp: Morrie Ryskind & Anthony Veiller, b/o play by Edna Ferber & George S. Kaufman. Cast: Ginger Rogers, Adolphe Menjou, Gail Patrick, Constance Collier, Andrea Leeds, Lucille Ball, Eve Arden, Jack Carson, Ann Miller. Among stage-struck girls, KH is self-confident debutante who becomes a star.

14. BRINGING UP BABY. RKO, 1938. *Howard Hawks*. Sp: Dudley Nichols & Hagar Wilde, b/o story by Wilde. Cast: Cary Grant, Charles Ruggles, May Robson, Walter Catlett, Barry Fitzgerald, Fritz Feld, Jack Carson. KH is daffy heiress who sets her sights on absent-minded zoology professor.

15. HOLIDAY. Columbia, 1938. *George Cukor*. Sp: Donald Ogden Stewart & Sidney Buchman, b/o play by Philip Barry. Cast: Cary Grant, Doris Nolan, Lew Ayres, Edward Everett Horton, Binnie Barnes, Jean Dixon. KH is wealthy but practical girl who wins her snobbish sister's fiance.

16. THE PHILADELPHIA STORY. MGM, 1940. *George Cukor*. Sp: Donald Ogden Stewart, b/o play by Philip Barry. Cast: Cary Grant, James Stewart, Ruth Hussey, John Howard, Roland Young, John Halliday, Virginia Weidler, Mary Nash. As wealthy Tracy Lord, KH learns humility, returns to her ex-husband. KH's third Oscar nomination. Remade as musical *High Society* in 1956.

17. WOMAN OF THE YEAR. MGM, 1942. *George Stevens*. Sp: Ring Lardner Jr. & Michael Kanin. Cast Spencer Tracy, Fay Bainter, Reginald Owen, Minor Watson, William Bendix. Noted columnist (KH) marries sportswriter. First of nine Tracy-Hepburn films. KH's fourth Academy Award nomination. Remade as *Designing Woman* in 1957.

18. KEEPER OF THE FLAME. MGM, 1942. *George Cukor*. Sp: Donald Ogden Stewart, b/o novel by I. A. R. Wylie. Cast: Spencer

Tracy, Richard Whorf, Margaret Wycherly, Donald Meek, Horace (Stephen) McNally, Audrey Christie, Frank Craven. KH as widow of famous American tries to keep crusading journalist from learning that her husband was a Fascist.

19. STAGE DOOR CANTEEN. United Artists, 1943. *Frank Borzage.* Sp: Delmer Daves. Cast: Cheryl Walker, William Terry, Marjorie Riordan, Lon McAllister, Ruth Roman. KH was one of 65 stars who contributed their talents to the wartime canteen run by the American Theatre Wing.

20. DRAGON SEED. MGM, 1944. *Jack Conway & Harold S. Bucquet.* Sp: Marguerite Roberts & Jane Murfin, b/o novel by Pearl S. Buck. Cast: Walter Huston, Aline MacMahon, Akim Tamiroff, Turhan Bey, Hurd Hatfield, Frances Rafferty, Agnes Moorehead, Lionel Barrymore (narrator). KH is Chinese peasant who becomes a heroic guerilla fighter.

21. WITHOUT LOVE. MGM, 1945. *Harold S. Bucquet.* Sp: Donald Ogden Stewart, b/o play by Philip Barry. Cast: Spencer Tracy, Lucille Ball, Keenan Wynn, Carl Esmond, Patricia Morison, Felix Bressart, Gloria Grahame. KH is widow who enters into a platonic marriage with bachelor scientist.

22. UNDERCURRENT. MGM, 1946. *Vincente Minnelli.* Sp: Edward Chodorov, b/o story *You Were There* by Thelma Stradel. Cast: Robert Taylor, Robert Mitchum, Edmund Gwenn, Marjorie Main, Jayne Meadows. KH is small-town girl who marries a moody psychopath.

23. THE SEA OF GRASS. MGM, 1947. *Elia Kazan.* Sp: Marguerite Roberts & Vincent Lawrence, b/o novel by Conrad Richter. Cast: Spencer Tracy, Melvyn Douglas, Phyllis Thaxter, Robert Walker, Edgar Buchanan, Harry Carey. Western drama with KH as wife of cattle baron.

24. SONG OF LOVE. MGM, 1947. *Clarence Brown.* Sp: Ivan Tors, Ermgard Von Cube, Allen Vincent & Robert Ardrey, b/o play by Bernard Schubert & Mario Silva. Cast: Paul Henreid, Robert Walker, Leo G. Carroll, Henry Daniell, Gigi Perreau. KH is Clara Wieck Schumann in this biography of the Schumanns

and their friend Johannes Brahms.

25. STATE OF THE UNION. MGM, 1948. *Frank Capra*. Sp: Anthony Veiller & Myles Connolly, b/o play by Howard Lindsay and Russel Crouse. Cast: Spencer Tracy, Van Johnson, Angela Lansbury, Adolphe Menjou, Lewis Stone. KH as the estranged wife of a candidate for President of the United States who helps him see that he is being used by crooked politicians.

26. ADAM'S RIB. MGM, 1949. *George Cukor*. Sp: Garson Kanin & Ruth Gordon. Cast: Spencer Tracy, Judy Holliday, Tom Ewell, David Wayne, Jean Hagen, Hope Emerson. Lawyer (KH) clashes with her assistant DA husband in trial.

27. THE AFRICAN QUEEN. Horizon-Romulus/United Artists, 1951. (c) *John Huston*. Sp: John Huston & James Agee, b/o novel by C. S. Forester. Cast: Humphrey Bogart, Robert Morley, Peter Bull, Theodore Bikel. Prim missionary (KH) allies with hard-drinking adventurer in Africa during World War I. Her fifth Oscar nomination.

28. PAT AND MIKE. MGM, 1952. (c) *George Cukor*. Sp: Garson Kanin & Ruth Gordon. Cast: Spencer Tracy, Aldo Ray, William Ching, Sammy White, George Mathews, Loring Smith. KH is talented athlete who catches the eye of a sports promoter.

29. SUMMERTIME. Lopert Films/United Artists, 1955. (c) *David Lean*. Sp: David Lean & H. E. Bates, b/o play *The Time of the Cuckoo* by Arthur Laurents. Cast: Rossano Brazzi, Isa Miranda, Darren McGavin, Mari Aldon, Jane Rose. Middle-aged spinster (KH) finds romance in Venice. KH's sixth Academy Award nomination.

30. THE RAINMAKER. Paramount, 1956. (c) *Joseph Anthony*. Sp: N. Richard Nash, b/o his play. Cast: Burt Lancaster, Wendell Corey, Lloyd Bridges, Earl Holliman, Cameron Prud'Homme. Old maid Lizzie Curry (KH) is brought out of her shell by a con-man. KH's seventh Oscar nomination.

31. THE IRON PETTICOAT. MGM, 1956. (c) *Ralph Thomas*. Sp: Ben Hecht (uncredited), b/o story by Harry Saltzman (actually Ben Hecht). Cast: Bob Hope, James Robertson Justice, Rob-

ert Helpmann, David Kossoff. KH is Russian Air Force captain who is won over to capitalism by an American pilot.

32. DESK SET. 20th Century-Fox, 1957. (c) *Walter Lang.* Sp: Phoebe & Henry Ephron, b/o play by William Marchant. Cast: Spencer Tracy, Gig Young, Joan Blondell, Dina Merrill, Sue Randall, Neva Patterson. Comedy of reference librarian (KH), a methods engineer, and an electronic brain.

33. SUDDENLY, LAST SUMMER. Horizon/Columbia Pictures, 1959. *Joseph L. Mankiewicz.* Sp: Gore Vidal & Tennessee Williams, b/o play by Williams. Cast: Elizabeth Taylor, Montgomery Clift, Albert Dekker, Mercedes McCambridge. KH is eccentric millionairess who tries to prevent her niece from recounting the horrible circumstances of her son's death. Her eighth Oscar nomination.

34. LONG DAY'S JOURNEY INTO NIGHT. Ely Landau/Embassy Pictures, 1962. *Sidney Lumet.* Sp: Eugene O'Neill, b/o his play. Cast: Ralph Richardson, Jason Robards Jr., Dean Stockwell, Jeanne Barr. KH is the drug-ridden mother in the author's autobiographical play. Academy Award nomination nine for KH.

35. GUESS WHO'S COMING TO DINNER. Columbia, 1967. (c) *Stanley Kramer.* Sp: William Rose. Cast: Spencer Tracy, Sidney Poitier, Katharine Houghton, Cecil Kellaway, Beah Richards, Roy Glenn Sr. KH and Tracy are liberal parents whose standards are tested when their daugher plans to marry a black doctor. KH's second Academy Award.

36. THE LION IN WINTER. Avco-Embassy, 1968. (c) *Anthony Harvey.* Sp: James Goldman, b/o his play. Cast: Peter O'Toole, Jane Merrow, John Castle, Timothy Dalton, Anthony Hopkins, Nigel Stock. KH as Eleanor of Aquitaine, wife of King Henry II. An unprecedented third Oscar for KH (shared with Barbra Streisand).

37. THE MADWOMAN OF CHAILLOT. Ely Landau/Commonwealth-United, 1969. (c) *Bryan Forbes.* Sp: Edward Anhalt, b/o play by Jean Giraudoux. Cast: Charles Boyer, Claude Dauphin, Edith Evans, Paul Henreid, Oscar Homolka, Margaret Leighton, Giulietta Masina, Yul Brynner, Richard Chamberlain, Danny

Kaye. Eccentric countess (KH) battles a large cartel in Paris.

38. THE TROJAN WOMEN. Cinerama, 1971. (c) *Michael Cacoyannis.* Sp: Michael Cacoyannis, b/o Edith Hamilton's translation of the play by Euripides. Cast: Vanessa Redgrave, Genevieve Bujold, Irene Papas. KH is Hecuba, Queen of Troy, reduced to slavery by the Greeks.

39. A DELICATE BALANCE. Ely Landau/American Film Theatre, 1973. *Tony Richardson.* Sp: Edward Albee, b/o his play. Paul Scofield, Lee Remick, Kate Reid, Joseph Cotten, Betsy Blair. KH is a neurotic, soul-baring wife and mother of an alcoholic daughter and friend of frightened neighbors who move in on the family.

OTHER FILM APPEARANCES BY KATHARINE HEPBURN

WOMEN IN DEFENSE. OWI, 1941. KH delivered the narration written by Eleanor Roosevelt in this one-reel short about women's contribution to the war effort.

THE AMERICAN CREED. Selznick, 1946. *Robert Stevenson.* Two-reel trailer for American Brotherhood Week. KH appeared with Ingrid Bergman, Eddie Cantor, Van Johnson, James Stewart, Shirley Temple, Jennifer Jones, Edward G. Robinson, and Walter Pidgeon.

Untitled trailer for American Cancer Society. 1946. KH and Spencer Tracy made a plea for contributions in this one-reeler.

SOME OF THE BEST. MGM, 1949. Forty-minute promotional film celebrating MGM's Silver Anniversary, narrated by Lionel Barrymore. Among clips from twenty-four films from the studio archives and from eighteen forthcoming films were scenes from *The Philadelphia Story* and *Adam's Rib* with KH.

STAGE APPEARANCES
BY KATHARINE HEPBURN

THE CZARINA by Melchior Lengyel and Lajos Biro. Baltimore, Maryland, Summer, 1928

THE CRADLE SNATCHERS by Russell Medcraft and Norma Mitchell. Baltimore, Maryland. Summer, 1928.

THE BIG POND by George Middleton and A.E. Thomas. Great Neck, Long Island. 1928. KH dismissed after one performance.

THESE DAYS by Katharine Clugston. Cort Theatre, New York City. November 12, 1928. Play ran for eight performances.

HOLIDAY by Philip Barry. Plymouth Theatre, New York City. November 26, 1928. KH understudied Hope Williams as Linda Seton, subsequently played the part once in national company.

DEATH TAKES A HOLIDAY by Alberto Casella. Adelphi Theatre, Philadelphia. November 25, 1929. KH replaced by Rose Hobart before Broadway opening.

A MONTH IN THE COUNTRY by Ivan Turgenev. Guild Theatre, New York City. March 17, 1930. KH understudied one role, later played another.

A ROMANTIC YOUNG LADY by G. Martinez Sierra. The Berkshire Playhouse. Stockbridge, Massachusetts. Summer, 1930.

THE ADMIRABLE CRICHTON by Sir James M. Barrie. The Berkshire Playhouse. Stockbridge, Massachusetts. Summer, 1930.

ART AND MRS. BOTTLE, OR THE RETURN OF THE PURI-TAN by Benn W. Levy. Maxine Elliott Theatre, New York City. November 18, 1930.

JUST MARRIED by Adelaide Matthews and Anne Nichols. The Ivoryton Players, Ivoryton, Connecticut. Summer, 1931.

THE CAT AND THE CANARY by John Willard. The Ivoryton Players, Ivoryton, Connecticut, Summer, 1931.

THE MAN WHO CAME BACK by Jules Eckert Goodman. The Ivoryton Players, Ivoryton, Connecticut. Summer, 1931.

THE ANIMAL KINGDOM by Philip Barry. Pittsburgh and Boston. December, 1931. KH replaced by Frances Fuller before Broadway opening.

THE WARRIOR'S HUSBAND by Julian Thompson. Morosco Theatre, New York City. March 11, 1932.

THE BRIDE THE SUN SHINES ON by Will Cotton. Ossining, New York. Summer, 1932.

THE LAKE by Dorothy Massingham and Murray MacDonald. Martin Beck Theatre, New York City. December 26, 1933.

JANE EYRE by Charlotte Bronte. New Haven, Connecticut. December 26, 1936. KH played Jane Eyre on tour ending in Baltimore on April 3, 1937.

THE PHILADELPHIA STORY by Philip Barry. Shubert Theatre, New York City. March 28, 1939. KH played Tracy Lord through March, 1940 and toured in the national company during the 1940-41 season.

WITHOUT LOVE by Philip Barry. St. James Theatre, New York City. November 10, 1942.

AS YOU LIKE IT by William Shakespeare. Cort Theatre, New York City. January 26, 1950. KH also played Rosalind on subsequent national tour.

THE MILLIONAIRESS by George Bernard Shaw. New Theatre, London. June 27, 1952. Also Shubert Theatre, New York City. October 10, 1952.

THE TAMING OF THE SHREW/MEASURE FOR MEASURE/THE MERCHANT OF VENICE by William Shakespeare. The Old Vic Company tour of Australia. Summer, 1955. KH played Katharina, Isabella, and Portia respectively.

THE MERCHANT OF VENICE by William Shakespeare. American Shakespeare Festival Theatre, Stratford, Connecticut. July 10, 1957. KH played Portia.

MUCH ADO ABOUT NOTHING by William Shakespeare. American Shakespeare Festival Theatre, Stratford, Connecticut. August 3, 1957. KH played Beatrice.

TWELFTH NIGHT by William Shakespeare. American Shakespeare Festival Theatre, Stratford, Connecticut. June 3, 1960. KH played Viola.

ANTONY AND CLEOPATRA by William Shakespeare. American Shakespeare Festival Theatre, Stratford, Connecticut, July 22, 1960. KH played Cleopatra.

COCO by Alan Jay Lerner (lyrics by Alan Jay Lerner and music by Andre Previn). Mark Hellinger Theatre, New York City. December 18, 1969. KH played Coco Chanel for nine months on Broadway and in the national company beginning in Cleveland on January 11, 1971.

KATHARINE HEPBURN ON RADIO

A MARRIAGE HAS BEEN ARRANGED with Adolphe Menjou. The Standard Brands Hour, NBC, June 1, 1933.

A FAREWELL TO ARMS with Orson Welles & Mercury Theater Players. Campbell Soup Playhouse, CBS, December 30, 1938.

SUFFER LITTLE CHILDREN (Special featuring two Biblical playlets written and directed by Arch Oboler. KH starred in one, Burgess Meredith in the other.) NBC, June 25, 1939.

THE PHILADELPHIA STORY (scene). New York Film Critics Award Program, NBC, January 5, 1941.

THE PHILADELPHIA STORY with Cary Grant, James Stewart, Ruth Hussey and Virginia Weidler. Lux Radio Theatre, CBS, July 20, 1942.

WOMAN OF THE YEAR with Spencer Tracy. Screen Guild Players, CBS, April 19, 1943.

THE PHILADELPHIA STORY with Shirley Booth, Lenore Lonergan, Vera Allen, Nicholas Joy. Arthur Hopkins Presents, NBC, May 19, 1944.

LITTLE WOMEN with Oscar Homolka, John Davis Lodge, Elliott Reid. Theatre Guild on the Air, ABC, December 23, 1945.

THE PHILADELPHIA STORY with Cary Grant and James Stewart. Screen Guild Players, CBS, March 17, 1947.

THE RIGHT TO LIVE with Dana Andrews. (Special program for United Jewish Appeal) NBC, May 18, 1947.

UNDERCURRENT with Robert Taylor. Lux Radio Theatre, CBS, October 6, 1947.

LITTLE WOMEN with Paul Lukas. Theatre Guild on the Air, ABC, December 21, 1947.

THE GAME OF LOVE AND DEATH with Paul Henreid and Claude Rains. Theatre Guild on the Air, NBC, January 2, 1949.

INDEX

(Page numbers italicized indicate photographs)

154

ABOUT THE AUTHOR

Alvin H. Marill is a New Englander by birth, a writer by profession, and an inveterate moviegoer by habit. He has written film and book criticism over the years for various newspapers, broadcast media, and entertainment publications and is a frequent contributor to film journals. He is co-author of *The Cinema of Edward G. Robinson* and a series of pictorial studies, focusing on such stars as Boris Karloff and Errol Flynn. He lives in New Jersey with his wife and two sons.

ABOUT THE EDITOR

Ted Sennett has been attending and enjoying movies since the age of two. He has written about films for magazines and newspapers, and is the author of *Warner Brothers Presents,* a survey of the great Warners films of the thirties and forties. A publishing executive, he lives in New Jersey with his wife and three children.